A HYPOTHESIS

Chapter 1   5

ASYNCHRONICITY

…the mesmerising simultaneity of aliveness
and deadness in a baleen whale corpse…

Chapter 2   25

REHEARSAL

…the awkward interiority of Descartes
doubting away his body, with a blanket
wrapped around his knees to keep warm…

Chapter 3   51

THE PRESENT TENSE

…the vibrancy of a tiny grandmother
dribbling basketballs or moving wardrobes…

Chapter 4   77

UNDETECTABILITY

…an incisor tooth poking through a child's gum
and a self-organised school, or…

Chapter 5   93

DURATION

…interrupted dictation after the collapse
of a global financial system.

---

* Five essays, serially published in Mousse Magazine, 2022–23.

Note:
Besides an extensive annotation by the author, following their initial publication, these essays have been minimally edited, with the exception of the word "cartography."[1]

This word, previously used to describe *all* five essays, has come to be replaced by the words "anatomical study,"
"conversation,"
"pile of clothes,"
"ecology," and
"spillage."

1. "Power relations act simultaneously as the most 'external', collective, social phenomenon and also the most intimate or 'internal' ones. Or, rather, power is the process that flows incessantly in between the most 'external' and 'internal' forces. As Foucault taught us, power is a situation or a process, not an object or an essence. Subjectivity is the effect of these constant flows of in-between power connections. This produces a methodology that is very important for nomadic thought: the cartographic method. A *cartography* is a theoretically based and politically informed reading of the process of power relations. It fulfils the function of providing both exegetical tools and creative, theoretical alternatives, so as to assess the impact of material and discursive conditions upon our embodied and embedded subjectivity.[...] One has to start from micro-instances of embodied and embedded self and the complex web of social relations that compose subject positions. As feminists say: one has to think global, but act local." Rosi Braidotti, *Nomadic Theory: The Portable Rosi Braidotti* (New York: Columbia, 2012), 4.

A HYPOTHESIS OF RESISTANCE

CHAPTER 1

This is an essay on

ASYNCHRONICITY

It is less like an essay, more like an anatomical study. Parts may or may not sync up, we will see.

The study begins between the kidneys and the hips, in a large muscle attached to the thoracic spine, just along the lumbar. The muscle runs from the spine to the legs, connecting the top part of the body to the bottom. You could say: this is the muscle that allows ears to meet hips, and jaws to meet livers. It is a mysterious agent, quite unfathomable. Most people don't know they have one, since developing an awareness of this muscle is not easy. Unlike surface muscles—a quad, a bicep—which pop out and publicise their presence, this one cannot be flexed and it cannot be released; it is called the *psoas major*.[2]
Located in the deep core of the body, the psoas is a complex communication switchboard. It transports and facilitates interactions between body parts by supporting the flow of blood, hormones, nerve messages, emotions, and energy. Such flow depends on the psoas remaining lively and loose—that is to say, it must stay long, soft, and spacious to allow substances and qualities to move around the body. Since the psoas is invisible to the naked eye, hidden beyond many layers of muscles, organs, and fascia, to locate it you must observe not the muscle itself, but tangible and visible symptoms it causes elsewhere.

---

2. Jo Ann Staugaard-Jones, *The Vital Psoas Muscle: Connecting Physical, Emotional, and Spiritual Well-Being* (Berkeley, CA: North Atlantic Books; Chichester, UK: Lotus, 2012).

For example, when the psoas becomes compacted, it causes stiffness in the hips, reduced circulation in the legs, locking in the lower back, an unwillingness to move, and diminished feelings.

> How can one study the emotional development of society?[3]

I wanted to walk this muscle into a meadow. More specifically, into an urban meadow in the German city of Aachen on May 5, 2022. This meadow is commissioned, managed, and studied by Dr. Martina Roß-Nickol,[4] whom I met in the meadow at a time of year when purple pioneer plants and a lot of dandelions were blooming. I wanted to ask Dr. Roß-Nickol what kind of time and management runs through a meadow, and what kind of time and management runs through a lawn.

Had I arrived in Aachen a few months earlier, the meadow would have looked neglected, even dull, with bare patches. During the winter, meadows are active primarily below the surface, where they "sleep"

---

3. Donald W. Winnicott, *The Family and Individual Development* (1965; repr., New York: Brunner Routledge, 2001), 230.

4. On May 8, 2022, at 4 p.m., in the symposium-like gathering *Asynchronicity*, at Ludwig Forum, Aachen, Martina Roß-Nickoll, professor at the Institute for Environmental Research, RWTH Aachen University, introduced her current meadow project "FLIP—Förderung der Lebensqualität von Insekten und Menschen durch Perfekte Wiesenwelten" (FLIP—Supporting the Quality of Life of Insects and Humans through Perfect Meadow Worlds). This was followed by "A Conversation on Meadows with Cally Spooner and Martina Roß-Nickoll," on the multitude of temporalities, species, and dimensions present in states of high biodiversity (including meadows), and how these differ from more intensively controlled and overused landscapes, particularly at the level of time.

in the soil. Later I checked the children's science and materials resource on *BBC Bitesize* and learned that soil is composed of 50 percent soil grain and 50 percent soil pores. Soil pores are the spaces in which air and water is stored. They are also the domain of tens of thousands of insects. Soil pores are an infrastructure in perpetual flux, since they cannot open themselves and so are entirely dependent on the constant movement of creatures such as earthworms to burrow holes, dig tunnels, open space.

> How can one study the emotional development of society? Such a study must be closely related to the study of the individual; the two studies must take place simultaneously.[5]

During the first hours, days, months of its life, an infant's psyche is not closely bound to its body, so a mother must hold the infant together to protect it from a feeling of falling apart. After some months the infant can hold itself together, and the mother shifts from absolutely important to relative. This change corresponds to a developmental journey: from double dependence (when the infant has no idea it is dependent), to dependence (when the infant notices the mother they depend on), to independence (the raging, desirous strivings of a toddler and, later, a teenager).[6] If infants are not held well, they might fall to pieces. To prevent them from falling they need to be held in a "facilitating environment,"[7] but I did not know this when my twins were born in the Rigshospitalet, Copenhagen, and I did not know the facilitating environment was me.

---

5. Winnicott, *The Family and Individual Development*, 230.
6. *Ibid.*, 8.
7. *Ibid.*, 27.

Three years later, I'm walking my twins home from the dentist. I'm holding my son's hand. He is fancy-dressed as a surgeon.

> It's not possible to do the right thing for a child by passing a law or setting up an administrative machinery

affirmed the paediatrician Donald W. Winnicott in 1965.[8] I knew this part about infant care, but I was surprised when the dental assistant said, "That was a great first visit for the twins!" That was a terrible first visit, I thought. They didn't let the dentist check their teeth.

There is very much I still do not know about infant care. Yet in the Rigshospitalet's maternity ward, I was the expert, better than anyone else, at holding my twins' emotional and physical needs because I was

> most likely to be quite naturally and without resentment devoted to this cause.[9]

In retrospect, "naturally and without resentment" feels untrue. Perhaps I've forgotten how 'unresented natural devotion' felt, or I came to resent the fact that I was a naturally devoted carer. In neoliberal Britain, where I was born in 1983, life instincts are of low value given that they are not useful to the performance of the free market. I needed to be a resilient British-born mother, so perhaps I rejected low-value life instincts, including natural devotion, since it is too risky to be socioeconomically powerless if you're British. Equally, if I reject such instincts, I could also take them back, identify them as knowledge, reclaim them with a feeling that "the sense of doubt is very close to its opposite which is belief, and to a sense of values, and to the feeling that there are things worth preserving."[10]

---

8. *Ibid.*, 76.
9. *Ibid.*, 6.
10. *Ibid.*, 76.

A baleen whale has died. It's fallen to the ocean floor.[11] Cold temperatures create an oceanic time delay, preserving the whale's body, slowing decomposition. The delay enables many creatures to take up residence and sustenance in the whale. The event looks otherworldly. A diverse community of species is thriving in the corpse. The whale is dead, and the whale is living; and of course this is possible, as any shaman, any mother, any science fiction writer could tell you. It *is* possible to be in two states at once.

In Mark von Schlegell's novel *Mercury Station* (2009), time-travel sceptic and prisoner Eddard J. Ryan—incarcerated in a high-security prison on Mercury in the year 2150—must confront his doubts.[12] His former boss, Count Reginald Simwe Skaw, appears to have travelled to the European Middle Ages, possibly using Ryan's body as a means of transport, but Ryan cannot remember leaving Mercury. This is the mysterious practice of chrononautics: "the harvesting of times sexual organs,"

11. On May 8, 2022, at 3 p.m., in *Asynchronicity*, Ludwig Forum, Aachen, Dana Luciano presented her talk "Oceanic Time and Black Feminist Futures," bringing the undersea paintings of the US multimedia artist Ellen Gallagher in dialogue with what has been called the "oceanic turn" in contemporary Black feminist theory. Gallagher's work, in its highly textured cross-referentiality, moves across the dimensions of what Jayna Brown calls the "dimensional present," negotiating its histories and proliferating its possibilities. Drawing on Herman Melville's Moby-Dick (1851) as well as the writings of Octavia E. Butler, Gallagher aligns oceanic time and Afrofuturism, envisioning how bygone figures of the deep—from the discarded Black bodies of the Middle Passage to the ecologies formed from the corpses of whales—might help us to imagine life anew. Luciano joined on Zoom.
12. On May 7, 2022, at 2:30 p.m., in *Asynchronicity*, Kölnischer Kunstverein, Cologne, Mark von Schlegell presented "Chrononautics, Then and Now," a talk in which he reflected upon his own science-fiction experiences with time travel, including those contained in his 2009 novel *Mercury Station*.

the ignition of time bombs into history that send "back-
ward-moving waves forward into time" to "blow old
memories away."[13] Via a haphazard verbal joust with
his jailers (an artificial intelligence called MERKUR
qompURE), Ryan attempts to plug the gaping hole in
his memory, and incidentally shapes a thesis of time
travel as the *possible* transporting of an individual self
(with no vehicle, but something closer to 'flavour')
over and through time into another individual,
with support from a

> fragment of the original body, a good deal
> of energy, and a psychoactive campaign of
> epic proportions.[14]

The self becomes slippery. A chrononaut might accept
that all living beings comprise one evolutionary growth,
one living body, and regard the universe as its "phantom
limb," not a fact. Gregorian calendars and Greenwich
Mean Time become phantasmagorical, and everyone is
confused. "Let me out of this bedsphere," says prisoner
Eddard J. Ryan on July 5, 2150, at 17:30 hours SST. . .

> I need to make my own observations of the stars.
> . . . I want to stand out in the Gardens and check
> for myself that it's really the fourth of July.[15]

It is easier to destroy something than to maintain it,
and the best practice for maintaining a meadow is to
advocate that the meadow should never become a lawn.
A lawn is essentially a highly degraded meadow. A lawn
is, typically, a monoculture. They have low biodiversity
functions, are grown with a single crop, and are managed intensively with a lawnmower. When heavy ma-
chinery rolls over soil regularly, pores start to collapse.

---

13. Mark von Schlegell, *Mercury Station* (Los Angeles:
Semiotext(e), 2009), 46.
14. *Ibid.*, 92–93.
15. *Ibid.*, 105.

Some of the oldest soil in the world is a hundred and forty-four million years old. The soil in the United Kingdom is relatively young, around ten thousand years old, but it takes just a few minutes to compact it.[16] Once a pore has closed, it's very hard to reconstitute space, and the soil is left diminished. It's May 5, 2022, and I'm still in Aachen. In two months' time, says Dr. Roß-Nickoll, this meadow will also be mowed, to an insect-friendly height of ten centimetres. Annual mowing encourages a more diverse mix of flowers for pollination by preventing the meadow from being overtaken by aggressive, dominant species of grass. The meadow is largely self-organised, yet highly dependent on a gardener.

You'd think being a pinnacle of brilliance, an expert, *the one* who was *the most naturally* devoted, would stick in a mother's mind but Mothers are *also* very fragile, and—it turns out—very forgetful too. Although devotion is common, accurate devotion stories are rare. They are more or less unpublishable because they are, naturally, largely without drama. A devotional story would have very few characters—infants, facilitating environments, no plot, inaction, unexpected methods of timekeeping. But the stories are forgotten, barely written.

It's 1964, and Winnicott is discussing the psychoanalytical "fear of woman,"[17] but the noun could be

---

16. UK Parliament, "Introduction: The Importance of Soil to Society," *Parliamentary Business* (London: UK Parliament, 2015), https://publications.parliament.uk/pa/cm201617/cmselect/cmenvaud/180/18004.htm.
17. "This is quite different from saying that an individual fears a particular woman. This fear of women is a powerful agent in society structure, and it is responsible for the fact that in very few societies does a woman hold the political reins. It is also responsible for the immense amount of cruelty to women, which can be found in customs that are accepted by almost all civilizations." Winnicott, *The Family and Individual Development*, 242.

exchanged for "mother." He notes that in the history of every individual who develops reasonably "well,"

> there is a debt to a [woman]—the woman
> who was devoted to that individual as an infant,
> and whose devotion was absolutely essential
> for that individual's healthy development.

But, he continues,

> the original dependence is not remembered,
> and therefore the debt is not acknowledged,
> except insofar as fear of [woman] represents
> the first stage of this acknowledgment."[18]

It seems that patriarchy gives mothers amnesia, preventing them from writing history, leaving gaps.

After scavengers have consumed the whale's flesh, mollusks and crustaceans begin to feed on the bones and the leftover blubber. Next, almost two hundred different species move into the carcass and take up residence in and between the bones. They form a thriving macroscopic community that can maintain itself for fifty years.

> The law of excluded middle is a venerable old
> law of logic. But much can be said against its
> claim that everything must be either true or false

wrote Rosmarie Waldrop in 1993.[19]

---

18. *Ibid.*, 241–42.

19. Rosmarie Waldrop, *Lawn of Excluded Middle* (New York: Tender Buttons books, 1993), 68. On May 7, 2022, at 1 p.m. and 6 p.m., and on May 8 at 2:05 p.m., 4 p.m., and 6 p.m., in Asynchronicity, Kölnischer Kunstverein, Cologne and Ludwig Forum, Aachen, "Rosmarie Waldrop's Lawn of Excluded Middle* read by Will Holder (vocals) and Paul Abbott (drums)" was presented as three fifteen-minute readings of three verses, to a maximum of six people. *Note (1993): 1. The law of excluded middle is a venerable old law of logic. But much must be said against its claim that everything must be either true or false. 2. The idea that women*

The whale is dead? Yes. Alive? For sure. Logic is sinking, a world is forming.

Back at the Rigshospitalet, it's 2019, and timings are getting adjusted. Moving around at night, napping during the day, a mother and infants are experiencing their first temporal (and temporary) dislocation from civilisation. How long this continues depends on the mother, depends on the infants. This is hard to get used to, yet as Winnicott suggests (in response to overzealous paediatric care and stubborn midwifery in 1960s Britain), limiting medical interference (and advice) allows mothers to handle infants on their own terms, in their own time. A paediatrician should watch and learn from mothers while mothers watch and learn from infants, in a mode called "organised noninterference,"[20] not too different from how a gardener cultivates the meadow.[21]

---

cannot think logically is not so old venerable stereotype.
As an example of thinking, I don't think we need to discuss it.
3. Lawn of Excluded Middle *plays with the idea of woman*
as the excluded middle. Women, and more particularly,
the womb, the empty center of the woman's body, the locus
of fertility. 4. This is not a syllogism. 5. This is a syllogism.
6. Poetry: an alternate less linear logic. 7. Wittgenstein makes
language with its ambiguities the ground of philosophy.
His games are played on the Lawn of Excluded Middle.
8. The picture of the world drawn by classical physics conflicts
with the picture drawn by quantum theory. As A. S. Eddington
says we use classical physics on Monday, Wednesday, Friday
and quantum theory on Tuesday, Thursday, and Sunday.
9. For Newton, the apple has a perplexing habit of falling.
In another frame of reference, Newton is buffeted up toward
the apple at rest. 10. The gravity of love encompasses ambi-
valence. (Waldrop, *Lawn of Excluded Middle*).
20. Winnicott, *The Family and Individual Development*, 240.
21. "There are different definitions of benign neglect.
In terms of childcare it's about giving children the oppor-
tunity to develop at their own pace, without interference.
The word neglect is unfortunate because it's not neglectful,
it's positive, in that you allow a child to explore being

By the time my twins were two, they started to tell me about the difference between night and day. "The sun is up, it's morning now!" And "It's getting dark, it's night!" They knew the difference because I told them there was a logical difference: I needed *them* to sleep at night so *I* could sleep at night and be refreshed in the morning to work during the day. Implanting a wake-sleep cycle in an infant can be achieved by various means (for instance waking the infant from sleep during the day, so it learns to stay awake when it's light), but to any extent, a "rational" individual—one that has been encouraged to feel inactive at night and active in the day—is shaped and formed. This is mild timetabling and the moment when time sets to work on the body.[22]

independent, by not getting involved in every aspect of their life. I don't know whether you hear me when I often say to the twins, 'Call me if you need me.' You've probably also noticed there's a stage in a child's life where they're telling you to go away. But you're not being neglectful, you're on hand to step in if needed. A better way of thinking about it, although it's slightly different, is 'scaffolding.' You give a child something to hang on to, then they go off on their own, safely. I think it was a guy called Lev Vygotsky who introduced this idea of scaffolding, which is used quite a lot in schools now for independent learning. . . . The important thing about benign neglect is that [in] its benign-ness ... you neglect *to a certain extent*, but there is a baseline: the child is safe. It's the 'good-enough' parenting model: you've got a level of safety there in order for children to grow, develop, and explore ideas. But without that baseline, anything can happen, both at the individual and at the state level, too." Edited excerpt from a conversation with my mother, 2024.

22. On May 7, 2022, at 11 a.m., in *Asynchronicity*, Kölnischer Kunstverein, Cologne, Elizabeth Freeman presented "On Chrononormativity: Histories and Possibilities." In this talk, she introduced "chrononormativity," a term she coined in her book *Time Binds: Queer Temporalities, Queer Histories* (Durham, NC: Duke University Press, 2010), describing how time sets to "work on the body." Chrononormativity is an implantation technique, and

The "lines of acceptance"[23] regularly mowed around Dr. Roß-Nickoll's meadow confirms to the public that —whether abundant or dormant—this space is natural *and* cultivated. Regarding her infant, a first-time mother knows almost nothing while being the expert.

Freeman presented an example: how the segmentation of time begins (and is implanted as a somatic fact) when infants are trained to differentiate between day and night, often achieved through infant sleep training. Freeman additionally noted that while the segmenting of time began with sheltering from the night to sleep, and moving about during the daylight to procure food, she also cites E. P. Thompson, who argued that the fine-tuning of time might have begun with agriculture. However, this method did not fully co-ordinate (nor desire to coordinate) bodies to time, and thus to each other, in the precise, controlled externally instigated movements that exist today. When these precise, controlled, externally instigated timings and movements come to be considered innate and "natural" facts of the body, they start to constitute chrononormativity.

23. Who should place limits? A friendly gardener in North Rhine-Westphalia seems like a good bet, but the world cannot be run by gardeners. Actually, the world should definitely be run by gardeners. Imagine! It is really not fair to leave the burden with mothers. Or gardeners. Yet, having the State draw up limits poses "a danger to free society" (F.A. Hayek, *The Road to Serfdom*, 1944; repr.,London and New York: Routledge Classics, 2010, 52), an impinge-ment on seeing "how things travel when they are left alone" (Cally Spooner, *DEAD TIME*, 2018). Perhaps those lines of acceptance are moral, as much as aesthetic. I don't know. All I can say for sure is that the meadow in Aachen became *possible* because of its lines of acceptance. The matter of drawing lines, limits, is political.

Chrononauts "must have come, or might have come, but they never really came."[24] A whale is alive, *and* dead. Yet normativity is a mode of external regulation that makes *one* way of being seem like *the only*, "natural" fact. In the case of temporality, this singular way of being is *chrono*normativity. Coined by Elizabeth Freeman in *Time Binds* (2010), chrononormativity is "the use of *time* to organise individual human bodies towards maximum productivity."[25]

"Work on the body," at the micro level of timing, unfolds in the opening pages of Michel Foucault's *Discipline and Punish* (1975)[26]: it's 1757 and a prisoner is being executed. There's a dismemberment, a skinning; it's awful—it's going wrong, it's terribly inefficient. Foucault then time jumps eighty years to 1838, and the gruesome punishment has been replaced by a cleaner, less visual, but equally brutal means: a prison timetable. Citing articles Léon Faucher drew up for the house of young prisoners in Paris, Foucault relays the details:

24. Von Schlegell, *Mercury Station*, 48.
25. Freeman refers to something beyond people finding themselves with less time than they need; rather, she joins Foucault's thoughts on temporality as a disciplinary power—noting, as he does, that time is used to bind and restrict human flesh and its life-force—through regulation. "Binding turns mere existence into a form of mastery." Freeman, *Time Binds*, 3.
26. During her talk "On Chrononormativity: Histories and Possibilities," [see footnote 22] Freeman referred to *Discipline and Punish: The Birth of the Prison*, and drew attention to Foucault's juxtaposition of an execution in the 1700s and a prison timetable in the 1800s. The latter is a definitive implantation technique by which temporal, institutional forces come to seem like somatic facts. Schedules, calendars, time zones, wristwatches, and today push notifications might seem "natural to those they privilege." Yet, these manipulations of time "convert historically specific regimes of asymmetric power into seemingly ordinary bodily tempos and routines…" (Elizabeth Freeman, *Time Binds*, 3.)

A day begins at 6 a.m. and ends at 7:30 p.m. (summer) or 8:30 p.m. (winter). In between, every single activity, bodily function, and movement is acutely prescribed and timed. Articles include rising, working, eating, schooling, but also entering, exiting, handwashing, and standing in line. Held by timings and tasks, the prisoner's body is "broken down into its elements; the position of the body, limbs, articulations is defined; to each movement are assigned a direction, an aptitude, a duration; their order of succession is prescribed. Time penetrates the body and with it all the meticulous controls of power."[27] No longer torn apart, burned, or skinned, the body is moved by the timetable, dominated by being made *docile*. The day ends in article 28: back in the prisoners' cells, it is 7:30 p.m.: "At the first drum-roll they must undress, and at the second get into bed."[28]

It is not common for a mother to shatter infants into psychological bits and somatic pieces, but it is possible that the psyche and the soma might never knit together. Put otherwise: a connection between body and soul could remain loose and weak if an individual has not been sufficiently held. I wonder if I held my twins okay. I'm doubtful, given that there were two infants to hold simultaneously, or because I only yesterday thought to Google "how do I hold infants well?" If devotion is interrupted, if a facilitating environment did not *physically* hold an infant "well," then the infant's "frustrations" might not be felt by the infant with full intensity.[29] Perhaps a diminished capacity for rage, a diminished capacity for desire, diminished capacities to refuse dental visits or defend being constantly fancy-dressed as a surgeon.

27. Michel Foucault, *Discipline and Punish: The Birth of the Prison* (New York: Vintage, 1995), 152.
28. *Ibid.*, 7.
29. Winnicott, *The Family and Individual Development*, 8.

How can one study the emotional development of society? Such a study must be closely related to the study of the individual, the two studies must take place simultaneously.[30]

As Foucault maps it out, the temporalization and syncopation of bodies, as a disciplinary strategy, was honed somewhere between monasteries, factories, and schools, but the military borrowed tips from it too. Using exhaustion to extract from time "ever more available moments and from each moment, ever more *useful* forces," a state of control is achieved so that bodies are systematised, then moved in sync with other bodies.[31] This is propagated by (among other techniques) dividing bodies (pupils, prisoners, soldiers) into ranks. Such divisive groupings might be the origins of "the performance principle" in which society, per Herbert Marcuse in 1955, "becomes stratified according to the competitive economic performances[32] of its members."

---

30. *Ibid.*, 230.
31. Foucault, *Discipline and Punish*, 154.
32. In *Perform or Else: From Discipline to Performance*, Jon McKenzie describes the front cover of a 1994 edition of *Forbes* magazine: a man wearing a suit and tie has a walking stick hooked around his neck that threatens to pull him off the front cover of *Forbes*. Under his image are the words "Perform—or else." The image quotes both the corporate, immaterial labourer and a Vaudevillian cabaret technique in which a failing performer—booed and jeered by an audience—is "hooked" off the stage by a compère. In both readings—be it businessman or cabaret artist— a failure to perform results in redundancy. What follows is McKenzie's factual framing of "performance" asking questions as to whom, or rather *what* performs: "air fresheners, roofing insulation, bicycles, carpets and rugs, powerboats, wall coverings, drain panels, cleansing towels, car-stereo equipment, bakeware, aquarium filters, tires, fabric, window film, woodworking knives, automotive timing chains, foil containers, audio antennae, deep-fat fryers, embossing

Under allegedly improving societal conditions and with rapidly advancing technological progress,

> men do not live their own lives but perform pre-established functions.[33]

By 2022, the hard division Marcuse perceived between performing bodies, timings, the cogs of the machine, factory working hours, and a pitiful amount of leisure time might in some cases have shifted, for example, to a more flexible corporate place, but the status quo remains: I did not anticipate that a microphysical disciplinary power would determine my relationship to my children. Hip flexors stiffen, vertebrae compound, lymphatic drainage clogs up the calves, and time with children shrinks. As the individual sits in a chair to work, body and mind become less functional, less vital, and it seems somehow less possible to feel from the gut. No amount of encouragement from the *Harvard Business Review* to stretch and move every thirty minutes (because moving increases performance)[34] or from Beyoncé to "quit" ("Release ya job, release the time [let's go, let's go, let's go, let's go]")[35] can help. The issue is structural. Essentially the psoas is a shelf that supports internal organs, so that any muscular contraction it propels (say, when walking) can stimulate and massage the intestines, kidneys, liver, spleen, pancreas, bladder,

---

tools, mop handles, music synthesisers, casement windows, and eyeliners—to name just a selection of those products marketed in the US with some form of the word 'perform-ance' actually appearing in their names." Jon McKenzie, *Perform or Else: From Discipline to Performance* (London and New York: Routledge, 2001), 11.

33. Herbert Marcuse, *Eros and Civilization: A Philosophical Inquiry into Freud* (Boston: Beacon Press, 1974), 44.

34. Nilofer Merchant, "Sitting Is the Smoking of Our Generation," *Harvard Business Review*, January 14, 2013, https://hbr.org/2013/01/sitting-is-the-smoking-of-our-generation.

35. Beyoncé, "Break My Soul," track 6 on *Renaissance*, Columbia Records, 2022.

stomach, and reproductive organs. These internal
organs are referred to as viscera. Communication
from the viscera to the brain is called "visceral messaging," and due to its closeness to and contact with
viscera, the psoas plays a major role in transporting
stimuli from organs to brain and back again, facilitating what is most commonly called "gut feelings."[36]
In the earliest stages of life, an infant and a mother
do not necessarily correlate to logic; day and night
may have fallen out of sync, and Winnicott urges
his readers to be prepared:
> I must not believe that what mothers say to me
> gives an accurate picture.[37] I must be prepared
> to find the imagination at work, as indeed it
> ought to be.

He continues:
> What our experiences feel like to us, and the
> way they get interwoven with our dreams is all
> part of the total thing called life, and individual
> experience.

Or, to put it plainly,
> We're not just a bundle of facts.[38]

A baleen whale dies. It falls 3,238 metres and lands
on the ocean floor. Now, jutting up from the Pacific
Ocean seabed, there is a tunnel of ribs the size of a car.
Under this, a five-metre beam of spine. Farther along,
ethereal ventricles meet a rocky grey buttress of

---

36. Staugaard-Jones, *The Vital Psoas Muscle*, 75.
37. Following my erratic "Introduction" on February 17,
2024 at 10.00 a.m., to *A Thesis on Spillage*, a symposium-
like gathering at Graham Foundation, Chicago, and after
Ralph Lemon presented his "RANT" through an amplified
harmonica, jumping on the spot, ecstatically unsynchronised
with his collaborator, the dancer, Darrell Jones at 2.00 p.m.,
Lemon told me: "We are all unreliable people."
38. Winnicott, *The Family and Individual Development*, 161.

decomposing matter, then the baleen's rostrum bone, followed by a three-and-a-half-metre jaw. The jawbone is lined with keratin bristles that might look like sharp teeth, but this is the baleen's filter, a sieve. Keratin does not decay rapidly in water, especially not at 3,238 metres in fridge-like temperatures, so the feeding system stays as good as new. Now ten lilac-silver octopi are living on the whale. They are *Muusoctopus*, with bulbous heads the size of small footballs. They are wrapping their tendrils around whale bones, billowing in slow motion, floating at half speed. Some octopi are suckered to the skeleton, sprouting from the whale jaw, at times iridescent. Eelpouts glide around the skeleton, then nose-dive into the vegetable matter to eat softened bone. Reddish seagrasses are blowing, but every blade is in fact an *Osedax*, a boneworm. Thousands are lined up in rows, dissolving the skeleton into a ragged state. Hagfish snake into the carcass, like bendy pink tubes. A silver fish shoots up and out of the ribs. Another *Muusoctopus* reaches its lilac arm to touch the white baleen filter. It plucks the fine-toothed instrument with the tip of one tentacle. A hundred or more other species are present, too, but they're microscopic, inconspicuously integrated with the fabric of the whale. The event is Jurassic and futuristic.

It is possible to world-build while something is falling apart.

Back to the eighteenth century, the dream of a perfect society is typically attributed to jurists and philosophers. Yet

> there was also a military dream of society; its reference was not the state of nature, but the meticulously subordinated cogs of the machine . . . not to the primal social contract, but to permanent coercions.[39]

---

39. Foucault, *Discipline and Punish*, 169.

This vision of society was driven by an imperative: to forcefully *deny* that empires are subject to the laws of uncertainty, decline, or ruin. Such a vision does not hand down to individuals what mothers know, and what mothers are very often made to forget, namely: that devotion is asynchronous.

Or,

> Because I refuse to accept the opposition of night and day I must pit other, subtler periodicities against the emptiness of being an adult.[40]

---

40. Waldrop, *Lawn of Excluded Middle*, verse 5.

A HYPOTHESIS OF RESISTANCE

CHAPTER 2

This is an essay on

REHEARSAL

It is less like an essay, more like a conversation. Parts may or may not sync up, we will see.

It begins on the floor, in a body stretched out, facing up, head supported by three paperback books.[41] Fluid from spinal discs moves freely around the body. Hip joints, lumbar, and the vertebrae pop back into their places, shoulders relax, drop to the floor, widening. One arm pulls across the chest, then the other arm, wrapping the torso. Arms rise and fall, diaphragm takes air in, then sends it out. Since the psoas is resting in this pose, so too is the entire nervous system. Blood, hormones, and nerve messaging move around the body, opening up viscera to experience gut feelings, sending messages and spreading information from the jaw to the liver to the feet in an extrasensory dimension—a proprioception— a sensitivity to where a body finds itself in space and connects to its environment. In this case, the environment is the floor, but the body is less easy to locate.

In Western society, the perception of much of our bodies has gone missing. This loss is not accidental. It occurred because intolerable psychic conflicts are suppressed when an individual under-responds (and eventually fails to respond) to their instinctual needs. Such needs might have been obstructed and replaced by performance

---

41. This is the Constructive Rest Position, as described in Staugaard-Jones, "The 'Give the Psoas a Break' Exercise: Constructive Rest Position for Everyone," *The Vital Psoas Muscle*, 20–21.

principles,[42] principles that proceed, perhaps, from the chrononormative[43] swing of a pendulum clock in 1657, from the timely running of British trains in 1840, to the French prison timetable of 1838, to Hollywood's frame rates, to Instagram refresh rates—all regulating goods, images, prisoners, and people with a Western undulation, not natural to the bodies it holds and measures.[44]

42. *The performance principle*, coined by Herbert Marcuse, is a Freudian reality principle under which society becomes stratified according to the competitive economic performances of all its members, so that individuals do not live their own lives but "perform pre-established functions" (Marcuse, *Eros and Civilization*, 44).

43. Freeman, *Time Binds*, 3.

44. Pendulum clocks (c. 1637, via Galileo) were more accurate than the timekeeping devices that preceded them. All clocks, up until and including the pendulum, depended on natural phenomena—regular oscillation—derived from the Earth or the cosmos. Since a sundial or shadow clock could only work when the sun was shining, water clocks, candle clocks, and hourglasses were invented to support around the clock timings, yet their period of oscillation was likewise determined from acceleration caused by gravity, such as when the sand or water falls, thus making the Earth's rotation the "master clock" against which all clocks were calibrated. The construction of railways in the nineteenth century depended on the pendulum clock's gravitational swing working very, very well. Having different local times at each train station was confusing and dangerous, hence time needed to be highly synchronised, regulated. Very advanced pendulum clocks were developed and installed in public spaces, and named "regulators." The need for a single standardisation of the pendulum swing birthed "railway time" in 1840, and this new reality was delivered by Britain's Great Western Railway. It was gradually taken up by other railway companies in subsequent years, and timetables were standardised to Greenwich Mean Time (GMT). By 1855 time signals were transmitted telegraphically from Greenwich across the British railway network and by 1880 GMT became a unified standard time for the whole of the UK. Four years later, at the International Meridian Conference in Washington DC, GMT was ordained as the standard for any and all time

zones around the globe. The concept of *a second* was formally defined, then defined further into *fractions* of seconds. Pendulum clocks were eventually replaced by quartz clocks in the 1920s, due to the quartz clock's ability to measure this new micro unit of time. Yet, this new quartz power revealed that the Earth's period of rotation was not constant, and showed how inaccurate all prior clocks had been, since it made time gradually slow down, due to tidal friction, or the varying conditions of seasons fluctuating earthly rhythms in slightly unpredictable ways. Thus, the quartz clock revealed that the Earth (the master clock) was somewhat, unproductively, erratic. By 1955 a practical caesium atomic frequency standard was produced. This was designed to calibrate the frequency of a quartz clock in order to standardise it; yet, by revealing how the resonance frequency depended on environmental conditions, it also revealed the extent that the motion of astronomical bodies was also erratic. Transitions between discrete energy levels in well-isolated caesium atoms could provide a much more stable time-interval reference. Thus, International Atomic Time (TAI) arrived. Today, TAI is one of the main players in achieving a global, Coordinated Universal Time (UTC), the time scale used to determine local times around the world, enabling global travel, international trade, and transglobal communications. It dictates, globally, at what speed all clocks must tick. This discovery amounted to the death of the astronomical second, and the birth of atomic time (https://physicsworld.com/a/a-brief-history-of-timekeeping). Today, the presence of high frequency trading puts precision timekeeping centre stage and sets atomic time to work, enabling traders to almost predict the future. As former trader Michael Lewis says while being interviewed about *Flash Boys*, his book on high frequency trading: "If I get price changes before everybody else—if I know a stock price is going up or going down before you do—I can act on it. If you're coming in to buy shares in Procter & Gamble and you think the price is 80... and I'm sitting there as a high-frequency trader and I know that the price of Procter & Gamble is actually lower—it's gone down [to] 79—I can buy it [at] 79 and sell it to you at 80. So it's a bit like knowing the result of the horse race before it's run. . . . The time advantage of a high-frequency trader is so small, it's literally a millisecond. It takes 100 milliseconds to blink your eye, so

> Concentrate on your body sensation as a whole.
> Let your attention wander through every part of
> your body. How much of yourself can you feel?
instruct Perls, Hefferline, and Goodman in 1951.
They continue:

> If you believe that you have had complete success
> with the above experiment, you were almost
> certainly mistaken.[45]

It's 1637, and "in the uniform lucidity of his closed senses, Descartes has broken with all fascination,"[46] setting off a powerful and enduring culture of distrust in bodies. We could map this back to astronomy, as Hannah Arendt did, pinning the distrust on the leaders of the Catholic Church, who lost their faith in Galileo, after Galileo lost faith in the earth being the non-moving centre of the universe. "And yet it moves," he supposedly said, as he watched the universe through his telescope lenses.[47] Yet the powerful men of the church were not pleased with what had been seen: their vision had been deceiving them, all along. The sensed, sensible truth of the external world was an embarrassment, and from this moment on, man would strive to be certain of

---

it's a fraction of a blink of an eye, but that for a computer is plenty of time." (Michael Lewis, interview by Terry Gross, "On a Rigged Wall Street, Milliseconds Make All the Difference," Fresh Air, NPR, April 1, 2014)

45. Frederick S. Perls, Ralph F. Hefferline, and Paul Goodman, *Gestalt Therapy: Excitement and Growth in the Human Personality* (London: Souvenir Press Ltd, 1972), 86.

46. Michel Foucault, *Madness and Civilization: A History of Insanity in the Age of Reason*, trans. Richard Howard (New York: Vintage, 1988), 108.

47. Mario Livio, "Did Galileo Truly Say, 'And Yet It Moves'? A Modern Detective Story," *Scientific American*, May 6, 2020, https://blogs.scientificamerican.com/observations/did-galileo-truly-say-and-yet-it-moves-a-modern-detective-story/#:~:text=During%20his%20trial%20for%20suspicion,end%2C%20truth%20would%20win%20out.

one thing: his own mind. This situation helped
Descartes prove his entire sensory organism to be
untrustworthy. Using his *Discourse on the Method
of Rightly Conducting the Reason and Seeking for
Truth in the Sciences*, he closed his eyes, plugged up
his ears,[48] and ran the show as follows:

> Since I found no society to divert me, while
> fortunately I had also no cares or passions to
> trouble me, I remained the whole day shut up
> alone in a stove-heated room, where I had
> complete leisure to occupy myself with
> my own thoughts.[49]

From his chair, with society comfortably absent,
Descartes used his mind to systematically doubt the
existence of his body and cognitively reason that the
physical world around him was false. In a toxic indem-
nity clause, which for some time became the foundation
of Western philosophy, he gained insurance over his
mind by sacrificing his unreliable body. Enclosing himself within *his* thoughts of *his Self*, he left out everyone
who knows the principle of sharing an environment
with a riotous toddler: *that* other, and *their* environment, can never be doubted away.

Because I have not, as usual, seen our twins since
9:00 a.m., and it is now 5:00 p.m., a gap between my
thirty-nine-year-old body and the twins' three-and-a-
half-year-old bodies has opened up. Now the twins are

---

48. Foucault, *Madness and Civilization*, 108.
49. René Descartes, "Discourse on the Method of Rightly
Conducting the Reason and Seeking for Truth in the
Sciences," *Discourse on Method* (1637), trans. and ed. S.
Haldane and G. R. T. Ross, first five parts (Cambridge, UK:
Cambridge University Press, 1911), https://www.marxists.org/
reference/subject/philosophy/works/fr/descarte.htm.

trying to smash this distance by running into the gap, and filling it with wrestling. The paperback books are gone. I am lying on two cotton mats, each 160 × 100 cm. We bought these mats for the twins to sleep on when they were four weeks old. We hoped that if they slept at ground level, they'd be able to roll themselves in and out of bed on their own, which would give us adults more time to ourselves while providing a place for everyone to fall asleep on the floor as and when possible and needed (which was very often). As we moved from city to city, we rolled up the mats, taking them and the twins with us, and this was our only furniture for maybe two years.

An infant who has not been held "well" might find their psyche and their body do not knit together and subsequently they might feel they are falling to pieces, or "falling forever."[50] Unexpectedly, as an infant matures, "holding them well" might also include letting the infants fall, a little. In the case of our infants, while the need to be held continues, well into the unknown future, they simultaneously developed a new emotional need too: to be thrown into the air by adult feet, precariously balanced at the top of fully extended raised adult legs, then dropped at great speed, to land on the ground, daily.

Now the sleep mats are crash pads. A toddler is balanced on raised adult feet, shouting commands, adult torso on mat, back shoulders or hip joints broadening from the weight of a toddler. Another toddler is scaling adult legs, waving a foam sword; sword falls with a cascade of jigsaw puzzle, adult vision is compromised: objects and toddlers are moving fast. A toddler drops from adult leg, toddler hands are pushed into adult eyes, adult nose used as foothold. Speed increases, toddler rolls over toddler, toddler thrown overhead; a play tent is turned upside down, it rolls across the mat with an

---

50. Winnicott, *The Family and Individual Development*, 26.

eruption of soft toys. Toddler climbs on adult head,
karate chops adult torso, toddler thrown off adult,
toddler pulled back, disappears, reappears under
duvet, dives, climbs adult legs to be thrown to the mat
with turbulence while remaining twin waits patiently
to board adult legs.

I had no idea I would play with children like this;
I thought we would be painting or bookbinding.

In the socioeconomic climate into which I was born,
and by which I was (somewhat) held—which was
Britain in 1983—there was a very bad encounter
between society and Margaret Thatcher.[51] She had
a dream: the dream was a highly free market economy
that would defund, dismantle, and privatise civic
situations and encourage competition. It procured
the maxim, now a cliché, uttered, not in parliament,
but in *Woman's Own* magazine:[52]

> And who is society? There is no such thing!
> There are individual men and women and there
> are families and no government can do anything
> except through people and people look to them-
> selves first.[53]

Then, later in the interview:

51. Conservative British prime minister, elected 1979 under
the influence of the publicist Keith Joseph and his connections to the Institute of Economic Affairs, London, a British
offshoot of the Mont Pelerin Society [see footnote 92].
52. *Woman's Own* is one of Britain's best-loved women's
weekly lifestyle magazines. It was first published in 1932. It
features news, opinions, "fashion, diet advice, health and
beauty tips, and info on what to buy—and what not to buy,"
interviews, "hot celebrity gossip," and real-life stories.
53. Douglas Keay, interview with Margaret Thatcher,
Woman's Own, September 23, 1987, https://www.margaret-
thatcher.org/document/106689.

There is no such thing as society.

Today, I am the logical consequence of this cliché.
Its climate is lethal to civic sensibility, to sacred space,
to that which cannot adequately handle and reason
itself solely by means of ultimate self-sufficiency, and
enterprise or portfolio management at individual and
collective levels. The cliché and its climate is particularly dangerous to that which is dependent yet has no
one or no thing to depend on. Yet most communal,
political, or utopic support structures are deemed econ-
omically irrational—since they obstruct the free market
flow—and will be surgically removed[54]. (I know this,
I saw this: I'm from London). The gaping hole left
behind fills up with the internally issued individual
imperative: *I will manage myself.*

"The strictness of mothers has an unexpected signifi-
cance," said Donald Winnicott in 1963,

> in that it produces compliance gently and grad-
> ually and saves the infant from the fierceness of
> self-control. By natural evolution, if the external
> conditions remain favourable, the infant sets up
> a 'human' internal strictness, and so manages
> self-control without too great a loss of that
> spontaneity which alone makes life worth living.[55]

54. In the 1970s and 1980s, when unions were striking
hard in the UK, bringing industry to a standstill, stagflation
ran high. Margaret Thatcher responded by razing the social
fabric. She privatised national industries, steel, and trains,
opened British industry to foreign investment, transformed
social resources and social housing into private assets, dis-
abled unions wherever possible, and rewarded entrepreneurs,
all within half a decade. Many commentators reflected on
her free market "structural adjustments"—for which she
claimed there was "no alternative"—as a civil war.
55. Winnicott, *The Family and Individual Development*, 16.

Having few regulations, and no limits, the free market compels individuals to self-manage by maximally extracting from selves, and others, at great cost to spontaneity. If the strictness of mothers can protect us, draw limits in a limitless place, perhaps our consciousness is in there—in the mother who provides protective boundaries from the fierceness of ourselves. Perhaps the consciousness begins, then, with mothers. But of course, if it falls to the mothers. Only the mothers are to blame. And I do not blame these mothers.

> Unless we recognize what we are asking mothers to perform in the world and for the world, we will continue to tear both the world—and mothers—to pieces.[56]

Like around 2.2 billion others, I am a mother. I also have a mother. She is a teacher, and a good-enough reader of Winnicott. Which might be one of the reasons why, in private, I was adequately held and why I thought I'd be good at craft activities. Besides her and my father, I also have a third parent: it is my socioeconomic-climate-parent, a shaper but not a great giver of life. The state of its home, as my formative home, is inadequate; it holds incorrectly. It's never read Winnicott and it's not good enough. A friend and I talk briefly about this theory, and she asks, "Why would you want a city to be your mother?"[57]

---

56. Jacqueline Rose, *Mothers: An Essay on Love and Cruelty* (London: Faber & Faber, 2019), 2.
57. "For British child development psychologist and paediatrician, Donald Winnicott, in 1956, holes arrive in a child as a result of environmental conditioning. That environmental condition is named by Winnicott: the moments when a child's giver and shaper of life is not a good enough mother. Harsh as this sounds, Winnicott is a sensible paediatrician. He assures us it does not take so much mothering to not poke holes in your child. As Winnicott says:

In the advanced text that he wrote in 1949 called "Hate in the Counter-Transference," published in the *International Journal of Psycho-Analysis*, in a passage on "A Mother's Love and Hate" Donald Winnicott noted eighteen reasons why a mother might hate her child.[58] Here are a few reasons from him, and a few from me: the baby is not the mother's own mental conception; the baby is not magically produced; the baby is a danger to the mother's body in pregnancy and birth; the baby is an interference with the mother's private life; the baby is a toddler, and the toddler is making the sound of a screaming kettle whenever it is presented with a football or a glass of milk; the toddler is smashing dents in the mother's human capital because the toddler makes the mother unable to *maximally* extract capital from many things, including herself; the toddler is throwing marbles in Pret A Manger during a badly planned trip to the United Kingdom, on which his mother over stretched him, and now the mother has taken him to a busy place to relax, which—fair enough —was a really

<hr>

Good enough is enough. Now I am not a mother. I also have a mother. She is a good enough reader of Winnicott. I have a second mother too. She is my financialised, socio-economic climate mother, a shaper, but not a great giver, of life. Her home is my home. She's deregulated and out-sourced. She's kind of insane. She's never read Winnicott. And she's not good enough." (Cally Spooner, *A Lecture On Stagnation*, Brussels: uh books, 2021, 10.)
58. Donald W. Winnicott, "Hate in the Counter-Transference," *International Journal of Psycho-Analysis* 30 (1949): 69–74, https://tpocambodia.org/wp-content/up-loads/2014/08/Winnicott-Hate-in-the-Counter-Transference.pdf, 73.

bad idea.[59]

59. Stretched beyond his and my limit, for maximum productivity's sake. Oh la la. I am trying to remember what
happened. I really cannot remember the forensic, ekphrastic
details, though. I think while I was overstretching myself,
trying to do too many things, working across too many
places, I pushed him too hard. I did not read his condition.
I am trying to remember. . . I think I'd taken the twins to
the UK, hoped to leave them there, then I would head on
to Copenhagen for work. But he was unsettled. The night
before I left, he wouldn't sleep. He stayed awake all night
crying, even though I was with him, in the same bed, as
usual. I think I was meant to wake early. I must have can-
celled the trip. I cannot remember, everything is always
such a muddle, when you split life across multiple countries.
     For some reason, Jesper was away too. Essentially
everything was moving underneath us, and we'd hoped we
could move twins, leave them at my mum's, and crack on
with work. But he couldn't hold himself together and so
he stayed up all night crying and furious and I was crying
and furious because he was crying and furious and we became exhausted and sick. I did not accept that his temperament is our shared limit, because I did not expect him to
express this temperament in this way, since until that point
he had always been fairly portable. I got angry, because
he was crying at night and I was tired the next morning,
so I dragged him and his sister out into Bracknell town
centre to eat a Brioche. I bought him some marbles in a
toy shop, I think. But all he really wants me to do is be still,
present, beside him while he works on his many complicated things that are too difficult for a four year old, and
back then a two year old, to muster. I *have* been available,
I have offered some parts but maybe not my full attention.
He breastfed until he was 2.5, I slept in the same bed as him
every night, because he would call out four or five times a
night to be fed, and it was easier to sleep in his bed full time,
in the end, but I would feed him while I was asleep and hence
I would not meet his eye. In the morning he'd kick me
because I was annoying him: I wasn't waking up and hang-
ing out with him, but I was tired. I wanted to sleep. He is a
fairly early riser. I was trying to hold the situation together.
The subtext to this is that there is a mother writing.

Alongside there is a partner, a father, who is the primary
carer, and the mother's attention is distracted because she
is writing and because she has twins to hold, and because
she lives in Italy, not England, away from her own mother's
child care and help, and because she is the one who has been
earning money and this is a burden because it has meant that
she has not looked her son in the eye in the morning, or the
day, or whenever because we are running all over the place.
But, I was always there physically, I would always, always
hold him. This son has a large amount of energy which is
unusual and erratic. It's not easy to hold and handle and
even when he was in utero he would not stop moving and
moving like entropy, like land mass, cascading and moving
and he would never stop. It is then no wonder that when he
is born he aspirates amniotic fluid into his lungs, and has to
leave us for hours and then, by the time he gets back, his
mother is already focused on how to hold another infant,
and how to hold schedules and how to hold herself together
and not fall apart so she can continue to make art/writing/
money. "The moment when the adult face fails or refuses
to play its part in the continuation of mutual gaze" says
Eve Kosofsky Sedgwick "is when, for any one of many
reasons, it fails to be recognizable or to be recognizing
of the infant who has been, so to speak, 'giving face.'"
She continues. "Based in a continuity of this circuit" the
effective communication with the "executive and coordinat-
ing part of the mother system is no longer maintained. This
creates a shame/humiliation response. . . presents as failure
or absence of the smile of contact, a reaction to the loss of
feedback from others, indicating social isolation and signal-
ling the need for relief from that condition. . . . Shame floods
into being as a moment, a disruptive moment." Head down,
eyes averted (him and me), throwing marbles (him) are
"the semaphores of trouble and at the same time a desire
to reconstitute the interpersonal bridge."

I have asked so many women, not all mothers, did I
fuck up in the Rigshospitalet maternity ward, Copenhagen?
And everyone says, no, no: you can compensate. So I will
try and compensate here by noting (in case he reads this,
one day) that his liveness is dazzling. Liveness is erratic.
I will list his liveness. His desire to be connected, to respond,
to feel things very deeply, to communicate, to kick the
air explosively just because, demanding to be taught

That is to say: a mother might explode, throw mobile phones, rip a toddler from the breast, dump a toddler on the sofa.

---

how cars or boats are built while he sits in the bath,
his mesmerizingly high speed, accurate dancing in the street,
in bed thrashing about all night because of dreams, perfection of wooden aeroplane construction, drawings made in
minute detail, sketching out fears as big squares and small
squares, desperate—URGENT—need to correctly identify
a puffer fish by its teeth, or send his laser focus to impossibly
complex tasks that need time, space, consistency to work
upon. And while he does not need someone to shove the
spatula in his mouth, he does need someone to remain
BESIDE him, just as I needed, REALLY NEEDED, my
mother and or father to sit by me for hours and hours and
hours while I focused on impossibly non-child-sized writing,
work, whatever. "*Beside* is an interesting proposition,"
Sedgwick says, " also because there is nothing very dualistic
about it; a number of elements may lie alongside one
another though not an infinity of them. *Beside* permits
a spacious agnosticism about several of the linear logics
that enforce dualistic thinking: non contradiction, or the
law of the excluded middle, cause versus effect, subject
versus object. Its interstate does not, however, depend on
a fantasy of metonymically egalitarian or even pacifist
relations, as any child knows who shared a bed with
siblings. 'Beside' comprises a wide range of desiring,
identifying, representing, repelling, parrelling, differentiating, rivalling, leaning, twisting, mimicking, withdrawing,
attracting, aggressing, warping, and other relations."
And then, I realise. This is a relationship. I would like
to write him a footnote so he knows that without his
relation (which I should remain beside, and hold/behold)
everything would be different, and I would not change
anything because all these messy tears and rages and
crushed brio aeroplanes, and bags of spilled marbles are
not meant to be walled up between "morose walls for
Sunday strollers and Monday intellectuals" (Maurice
Merleau-Ponty). And if the fate of those indirect gestures—
those complicated, visceral efforts—is to wind up stunted
and institutionalised, something has definitely been lost.

Winnicott wrote "Hate in the Counter-Transference" for analysts, to teach them how to respond to contradictory feelings that might arise in them in response to patients during a therapy session[60]. If the analyst suppresses these feelings, they'll create a disastrous masochistic relationship with their patient[61].

How to counter the transference of burdens passed from climate to parent, from parent to therapist, from patient to child? An analyst can learn from a mother who "has to be able to tolerate hating her baby without doing anything about it."[62] To tolerate being

60. To borrow from Andrea Fraser and her (masochistic?) relationship with the museum: "I can rip at the walls of my institutional body but I cannot leave it entirely. Because then I would cease to exist. Institutional critique has the texture of melancholia." Andrea Fraser, "Why Does Fred Sandback's Work Make Me Cry," *Grey Room* 22 (Winter 2005): 40. First presented as a lecture for *Artists on Artists*, Dia:Chelsea, New York, October 25, 2004.

61. On February 17, 2024, at 12.10 p.m., in *A Thesis on Spillage*, Graham Foundation, Chicago, Joshua Chambers-Letson, author of *After the Party: A Manifesto for Queer of Color Life* (2018), spilled a communion that does not leave our dead behind but draws them into the present. As he moves fast through pages of his paper, spilling each sheet on the floor once read, he showed us that healing a broken love object is a synthesis despite the incomprehensibility of melancholy and reparation. Presenting his own subjective unfolding—live—he showed why loss and death can be engaged in a mutually overlapping process, and that we might learn how to love and lose at the same time; how to undo and remake oneself through loss. When he says "we take our dead with us," Joshua means: we take the pathological, and work with it. A synthesis might arise when the practice of melancholia activates the political as a dynamic process that unfolds with both coercive and transformative potentials for the political imagination. That is to say, perhaps not forcing things into a reconciliation activates the political as a dynamic process that is both coercive and transformative? Both with limits of loss, of impossibility, along with the vibrancy and the melancholia of this knowledge… But it is hard to say for sure…

62. Winnicott, "Hate in the Counter-Transference," 73.

hurt so much by her baby and to hate so much
without paying the child out, and her ability
to wait for rewards that may or may not come
at a later date.[63]

By her example, an analyst thus needs to "display all
the patience and tolerance and reliability of a mother,"
and has to put their "own needs aside" in order to be
available, punctual, and objective.[64]

I *think* this means that intolerable conflicts and
capacities do not need to be so intolerable, so hateful,
if they are not *forced* into reconciliation; or if these
feelings are not resolved and dispensed with using epistemological *certainty*; but, to be honest, I'm really unsure.[65] *If* the condition of moving one step forward and
many steps back—*ad infinitum*—can be accepted by
therapist or mother, then perhaps this is the beginning
of an understanding: that the mother is not, unlike the
free market, free. This is the limit in the room: an understanding of "our bondage to one another—a mutual
bad debt to each other that we do not intend to pay."[66]
Always a parameter, always a *condition* that begins on
shared ground, but which never settles: it is a dependency that moves in more than one direction at once,
back and forth, which is able to move with vibrancy
because it does so *within limits*. It moves somewhat
democratically, since it needs to be constantly revisited
in order to thrive, in a state of infinite rehearsal.[67]

---

63. *Ibid.*
64. *Ibid.*, 69.
65. For an example of intolerable conflicts, see Andrea
Fraser [footnote 60].
66. Stefano Harney interviewed by Timothy Edkins, 2018,
https://www.youtube.com/watch?v=uJzMi68Cfw0.
67. In retrospect, "democratically" is not the right word.
On February 17, 2024, at 5.15 p.m., in *A Thesis on Spillage*,
Graham Foundation, Chicago, Irena Haiduk, director of
Yugoexport, a blind and non-aligned oral corporation initiated as a copy of the former Yugoslav apparel and weapons

Back from the UK trip, in our kitchen in Torino, tempers
continue to rage inside and out. I clatter about, cook
rice badly, make a mess. At my feet, someone has fig-
ured out her holding environment. Sitting in a cardboard box, with a soft-toy owl wrapped in a blanket
and tucked under her arm, our daughter reads a book
to the bird.

In Maurice Blanchot's *Writing of the Disaster*, which
I haven't had time to read, but which I googled,[68]
disaster "ruins everything while leaving everything in
its state." Or, depending on which translation you read,
"the disaster ruins everything, while leaving everything
intact."[69] (What a difference.) A state is not an ending,
it's a condition, and conditions shift and change. They
are constantly being translated, revised, and rehearsed,
no? They are not *entirely* intact. That is to say, whatever
the conditions there are to google, the search continues,
and (irrespective) both translations run like this:

> It does not wait for this one or that one, 'I' am
> not under its menace. By these means of saving,
> leaving (me) aside, the disaster threatens in me
> that which is outside of me, another me that
> becomes a passive other. There is no reaching

manufacturer Jugoeksport, inhaled thick smoke issuing
from the fallen buildings. Moments later, she exhaled
billions of zero-shaped smoke rings. From upstage (the
space of The Tragic) she opened her lecture with the following: "Trigger warning: I have never lived in a democracy."
Perhaps then, this is better: "not resolved and dispensed
with using epistemological *certainty*." OR "not *forced* into
a reconciliation" [from notes taken].
68. Roger Green, "Some Notes on Blanchot and Disaster,"
New Polis, May 27, 2020, https://thenewpolis.com/2020/
05/27/some-notes-on-blanchot-and-disaster-roger-green/.
69. Suchitra Vijayan, "Disaster Ruins Everything," *Polis
Project*, May 17, 2018, https://www.thepolisproject.com/
read/disaster-ruins-everything/.

the disaster. The one it menaces is out of reach, one cannot know if it is near or far—the infinity of the menace has in a certain manner broken every limit.[70]

The infinity of the menace has in a certain manner broken with every limit. Damn.

Here is a menace that seems infinite. Here is a menace that smashed every single limit, with a peculiar—almost mathematical—certainty. It is a cognitive *method* that maximises the capital and competition within every aspect of life, then renders the drive for maximisation as the omnipotent truth.[71]

Here is another menace that seems infinite: it is a peculiar kind of power, lacking exteriority. It is, hence, introverted, since it is led by the rationality that the highest common good is for individuals to limitlessly self-invest in ways that contribute to appreciation (or that at least prevent the depreciation) of their human capital. This includes measuring all possible inputs, "such as education, predicting and adjusting to changing markets in vocations, housing, health, and retirement, and organising its dating, mating, creative, and leisure practices in value-enhancing ways,"[72] then transforming these into "positive ROI—return on investment."[73] In ROI, the environment goes missing because ROI is a "cognitive concern of consciousness with its own content."[74]

---

70. Green, "Some Notes on Blanchot and Disaster" and Vijayan, "Disaster Ruins Everything."
71. For example, Silicon Valley is unregulated. It is able to exponentially and consistently boom. There are no limits and no laws. As foreseen by the Mont Pelerin Society [see footnote 92], "no limits" creates a state of competition, since businesses are free to maximally, relentlessly, spontaneously, and freely compete.
72. Wendy Brown, *Undoing the Demos: Neoliberalism's Stealth Revolution* (Princeton, NJ: Zone Books, 2015), 177.
73. *Ibid.*, 178.

Hence the disaster begins but does not end in the *self without a context*: a state in which everything is internalised—not well held, falling, and never landing—because the environment does not hold individuals, communities, traditions, values, intelligent democratic citizenship, or imagination. Nor does it provide a structure or a groundwork in which these can hold themselves. This sounds like a belief in "society," or in the state I'm also surprised I wrote that; I'm surprised because hardwiring from postwar neoliberal economics makes it normal to covet and cherish a disaster that begins but does not end in the state of this *internalised* performance principle,[75] which is an inadequate facilitating environment, ongoing.[76] Even neoliberalism's "critics" cannot see the extent to which we have

> lost a recognition of ourselves as held together
> by literatures, images, religions, histories, myths,
> ideas, forms of reason, grammars, figures,
> and languages. Instead, we are presumed to be
> held together by technologies and capital flows.

---

74. Hannah Arendt, *The Human Condition* (1958; repr. Chicago: University of Chicago Press, 1998), 280.
75. Terms like "the best performing . . ." or "worst performing markets" are real. For example, Credit Suisse is performing poorly because of the loss of public perception or persona for this bank, while Facebook stocks are "performing" well. Likewise: this rubric extends to the best-performing and the worst-performing individuals, too. Market-mentality becomes a microphysical power lodged within the bodies and psyches of individuals who are continually subjective to litmus tests of competition, across an enlarged domain of activity. An unending graph—a boom or bust environment—measures everything: stock value, currency value, credit score, how to live a better life, how many connections, how many links in a network, how many likes, how many patients are seen by a doctor in the shortest amount of time, how many school children pass a national curricular exam. This is a performance climate.
76. See footnote 57.

That presumption, of course, is at risk of becoming true, at which point humanity will have entered its darkest chapter ever. We would be the entities of human capital, and nothing else.[77]

When our twins were ten months old, I wrote a note on my phone that said, "I am entirely dismantled by my children." It was material, factual. I liked that note.

Since there was no toddler present in Descartes' enclosure, the trend in continental philosophy became an exclusive concern with the Self. This manifested in epistemic and rational attempts to reduce the world to "experiences between man and himself," Hannah Arendt tells us, referencing Descartes. But, of course, she never mentions the toddler. Now I'm reading the blurb on the back of *The Human Condition*, which was under my head. It's by Wystan Hugh Auden (italics my own):

> Every now and then, I come across a book which gives *me* the impression of having been especially written for *me*... The Human Condition belongs to this *small and select class*.
> — W. H. Auden[78]

I share the extensive criticism of Arendt in that she helped many such men of letters imagine their futures in the images of the past. Though, I still care for her accidental feminist move, which was to prove that Descartes took up too much space. "Patriarchy exercises its social dominance by taking up space as its birthright..."[79] says Legacy Russell in *Glitch Feminism*—thankfully not a seventeenth-, eighteenth-, or twentieth-century project

---

77. Brown, *Undoing the Demos*, 188.
78. Wystan Hugh Auden, on the back cover of Hannah Arendt, *The Human Condition*.
79. Legacy Russell, *Glitch Feminism: A Manifesto* (London and New York: Verso Books, 2020), 20.

—but one in which the full, intersectional contestation presented reveals the fullest extents of the systemic violences of the Western mind, gaze and its histories. Russell continues

> ...when patriarchy comes into contact with whiteness, it leaves little room for anything else.

Back in 1637, space was indeed taken up exponentially on many levels, one of which included the environment and context being swept away, along with those on the ground who were being held, or who were doing the holding.[80] His was a paranoid move; he felt more evolved in his context[81]. So he shut down the show for the sake of introspection.

I'd rather not go on, paranoid[82], about a six-hundred-

---

80. And I do NOT just mean mothers. I mean society, the social fabric, those who are doing the holding and the handling of life. Teachers, nurses, union leaders, et al., whose social work has been incapacitated by austerity measures that target those who hold and handle life. Any work that holds responsibility for the survival of lives, other than theirs and their family, as well as *anyone* supporting *anyone* with needs and dependencies, is swept away when a thought experiment arises that feels more evolved than its context, and refuses to engage with the outside world and its complexities. . .
81. Another example: at the preliminary meeting of the Mont Pelerin Society [see footnote 92 for context], hosted at the luxury Hôtel du Parc, levitating high above Lake Geneva, there were no social or civic bodies to block the sublime view. From their prime location, behind closed doors an elite group determined a competitive order that would shatter society irreversibly.
82. Elizabeth Freeman expands on Eve Kosofsky Sedgwick's concept of "paranoid criticism" as both the condition of having "the problem solved ahead of time, about feeling more evolved than one's context" (Freeman, *Time Binds*, xiii). Sedgwick's concept of "reparative criticism" stems from Kleinian reparation; a psychological process where someone repairs their inner world, where they can better

year-old archaic analogy/man/philosopher, though—
yet the parting of mind and body does still contain
the biggest question of all, one that feminists have
been contending with for so, so many years: if the body
is AWOL, banished, repudiated by cognition, sent
packing by a city, by an economic theory, by a fantasy
of the market, by philosophy, then how might we

> 'penetrate. . . break. . . puncture. . . tear' the
> material of the institution, and, by extension,
> the institution of the body?[83]

How might we ask: "*Who defines the material of
the body? Who gives it value?—and why?*"[84] Equally,
if the body is dismissed, then what of those bodies who
are handling other bodies, bodies that need to be

> held, to be moved, to be cleaned up, to be fed,
> to be kept at the right temperature, and to be
> protected from drafts and bangs. They need
> *their impulses to be met*, and they need *us*
> to make sense of their spontaneity.[85]

> When we give children the right kind of good
> time there is really an aim in it all, namely to
> make possible each child's own ultimate growth

---

merge with the shattering realities of the external, including
the love objects that one has done damage to. It's about
moving from the schizoid position—the reparative opposition
—to give the shattered self the chance to function within a
hostile world. Rather than controlling, surveying, and disciplining the object so it does not have the chance to leave me
—which is paranoid—it accepts that loss presupposes love.
83. Russell, *Glitch Feminism*, 25 with quotation from Jean-
Luc Nancy, "Fifty-eight Indices on the Body," in Jean-Luc
Nancy, *Corpus*, trans. Richard Rand (New York: Fordham
University Press, 2008) or, [see also footnote 60] "I can rip
at the walls of my institutional body…" Fraser, "Why Does
Fred Sandback's Work Make Me Cry?," 2005, 40.
84. Russell, *Glitch Feminism*., 9 [italicised in original].
85. Winnicott, *The Family and Individual Development*, 44.

to the adult state which collectively is called democracy,"[86]

wrote Donald Winnicott in 1964. I really didn't mean for this to be a twentieth-century essay, but I *was* born in Britain in 1983. And for seventeen formative years of my life and more, my body and the bodies around me were being inhabited, shaped, and prompted by post-war and nascent neoliberal economies. In the twenty-first century, we do not know, see, or hear any better.

In the mid-twentieth century, the pedagogue violinist and philosopher Shinichi Suzuki knew that a very young child, say aged three and a half, could learn to play the violin the same way they would learn how to speak.[87] Just as a baby learns to speak by listening to their primary carer, Suzuki believed the child could play musical compositions very well if they could first identify and create good tone, by listening to and with their parents. Tone is not limited to the notes; it's what occurs before and after, and Suzuki believes that a child can understand this by understanding how tone feels, physically. But if no one is interested in listening to a child's capacity for hearing and creating a good tone, the child may become tone-deaf.[88] Understanding this might be the beginning of building maturity.

Unusually: I've just picked our twins up from Ambra Bimbi day care because I wanted to correct my (normal? abnormal?) working-mother absence. Typically: my partner does the pickup. Our son seems confused by my presence, so he is emitting a constant high-pitched yet low-decibel scream, like a metal kettle boiling.

---

86. *Ibid.*, 30.
87. "About the Suzuki Method," Suzuki Association of the Americas, https://suzukiassociation.org/about/suzuki-method/.
88. "About the Suzuki Method."

The noise—coming from the corners of his mouth,
full of sonic attack, no vibrato—is telling.

If we try to manage our affairs normally—better than
normally—organismic self-regulation might shut down.
Good, basic examples of organismic self-regulation include going to sleep because we feel sleepy, or eating
something when we feel hungry. Resisting this—because reason says we ought to for whatever reasons
(usually work/deadline related)—is a condition of
Gestalt immaturity. If appetites and desires are not lis-
tened to, then the psyche is not fully connecting to the
body. If it has been held well, a child's body can be very
well connected to its psyche, and the child, in great maturity, can start to let its environment know what it
needs. I'm a bad listener, though. My partner pointed
this out subsequently, explaining that our son is not
tone-deaf. That low-decibel scream was a message—
he needed his environment to know that he needed
to eat: two Medjool dates, and a banana.

If appetites and desires are left to spontaneously regulate themselves, says Perls, Hefferline, and Goodman,
they can bring themselves into good order—*if* the individual can make contact with their body and their environment. I take this to mean: appetites and desires
might regulate themselves when they connect with their
dependencies. Within those limits, a state without epistemic certainty can be collaboratively *rehearsed* in an
ongoing way, and it might make psychic conflicts (and
the environments that contain them) less fierce, less intolerable. I'm hoping, then, that appetites and desires
can regulate themselves if they're *left to travel alone*, and
that, now and then, spontaneity might *land*, alongside a
greater perception of bodies. But lying on the floor, with
Hannah Arendt under my head, no kids till 5:00 p.m.
and thus three hours still to go before balances, weights,

restraints, and wrestling arrive, "regulate themselves
if they're left to travel alone" sounds laissez-faire.
A *performance* of unbridled self-sufficiency, cognitively
breaking every limit, free-falling into nothing. Or,
> a citizenry left to its (manipulated) interests
> and passions.[89]

Perhaps there is a way of removing the part in paren-
theses.
It really hurts to never land.

---

89. Brown, *Undoing the Demos*, 170.

A HYPOTHESIS OF RESISTANCE

CHAPTER 3

This is an essay on

THE PRESENT TENSE

It is less like an essay, and more like a pile of clothes. Things may or may not sync up, we will see.

It is widely believed that when her mother dies in 1941, my grandmother stops growing. From then on, she remains the height of an eleven-year-old. Thus my grandma is 135 centimetres tall when she emigrates from Reggio Calabria and joins her father, Domenico, in England.

Although we do not understand how he lands in England, or when he arrives, at some point between 1940 and 1945, Domenico, my great-grandfather, is held in a British prisoner-of-war camp near Godstone, Surrey. Southern Italian unemployment issues and familial complications are 1,432 miles removed from this county's parochial villages. I picture blue skies and English duck ponds. Domenico is fed cake. He catches the attention of an elegant British camp administrator. Her hair is immaculate, her heels are high. So I am told.

Before the war, Domenico travels back and forth between Italy and North Africa, on mysterious business, returning to Reggio with suitcases of lire. Coming from little money, he is prone to show off, then squander, any newly acquired funds. One day, at Napoli Centrale, while he waits for the train, thieves remove all cash and finery from flashy Domenico's suitcases, replacing it with old newspapers. So he claims. This kind of high-drama ad-hoc/cash-in-hand work dries up when the war begins, and is still dry when, freshly discharged from the camp in Surrey, Domenico returns to southern Italy and finds no work.

Back in Surrey, the administrator sends many letters to Reggio Calabria, each calling for Domenico to return to her. From Reggio, Domenico ponders his options. He reasons soundly: a country that feeds its prisoners of war cream cake is the place he would most like to live. And so, much to his late wife's family's despair, Domenico sells the family home, packs his collection of luxurious leather shoes, his silk cravats, his mandolin, and emigrates to the United Kingdom to marry. My grandma, still a minor, joins her father in 1947.

At this time, the Western world is responding in various ways to its war-torn symptoms. In places such as Britain, stability and growth are sought via socialism and Keynesian economics[90]. Elsewhere, Friedrich August von Hayek[91] invites thirty-nine liberals[92]

90. After WWI, support for (Keynesian) state "planners" in Britain were found at every end of the political spectrum, with the *Beveridge Report*'s bold plan to offer all citizens social welfare protection "from the cradle to the grave," garnering huge public support. The National Health Service, social welfare, and social safety nets were essentially the superstars of the 1940s. When it was eventually published as a book, the *Beveridge Report* reportedly sold more copies than any other publication that year. Members of the public waiting to procure a copy caused long queues outside bookshops.
91. Friedrich Hayek, an Austrian economist, naturalised as British in 1938, based at the London School of Economics. After his self-initiated attempts to support the war effort—via "an anti-propaganda writing project"— were rejected by the British government, while WWII raged, Hayek, frustrated, continued to teach and write.

His writing unfolded in a series of articles that became his magnum opus, *The Road to Serfdom,* a 400-page "anti-socialist book," which—after much hustling and forceful persuasion—was published and somewhat scathingly dedicated (by Hayek) "to the socialists of all parties."

Over its many pages, *The Road to Serfdom* argues that intervention from a state would undermine an individual's dignity, since implementing a centrally/socialist-planned economy would impede that individual's Freedom and Liberty (interchangeable terms for Hayek). Further, as Hayek saw it, state decisions on matters of investment and capital accumulation were theoretical, slow, regulation-bound, and thus bound to be wrong and fail, since the information available to the state could never rival the information contained in markets, which would always, he believed, be spontaneous and "true." Thus, to ensure markets (and truth) would abound, and to avoid slipping down a dangerous road to totalitarian socialist serfdom, it would be necessary to create a climate of "competitive order," an order of "reason" that would support markets above all else.

92. During his North American and European book tour for *The Road to Serfdom*, Hayek was able to network. His lectures were attended by numerous like-minded Liberals, who had been working in isolation after markets and liberalism fell out of academic and public favour with the Wall Street Crash of 1929. In April 1947, Hayek acted on his connections: at great expense and via complex transnational logistics, he invited 39 of these liberals to Switzerland, to meet in the Hôtel du Parc, Mont Pèlerin, over 10 days. The meeting was crucial for those invited. The central planning power of governments had expanded during WWII and their successful extensions of post-war social welfare programs, undid purely liberal ideas yet, like Hayek, those invited to Mont Pèlerin were staunch: they would systematically fight social and socialist planning for their entire careers. The meeting was co-chaired by the economist Milton Friedman, attended by the philosopher Karl Popper, the polymath-chemist Michael Polanyi, many more men, and—just one woman—the historian, Dame Veronica Wedgwood, plus Hayek's secretary, Dorothy Hahn. There were no school teachers, union leaders, mothers, doctors, or town planners invited to the meeting. That is to say, the room's social fabric was threadbare.

gather in the Hôtel du Parc, Mont Pèlerin, Switzerland, on April 1, 1947, to articulate a renewed vision of liberalism for the twentieth century and argue against collectivism.[93] Framing liberalism as a philosophy of 'freedom',the participants discuss, over ten days, the preservation of a free society by means of individual freedom[94], with growth and stability built on the

93. This renewed vision became neoliberalism—a biopower —that extends beyond the Liberal free market economy, and involves itself shaping the conduct of individual subjects. In *Undoing the Demos: Neoliberalism's Stealth Revolution*, Wendy Brown describes neoliberalism as "a peculiar form of reason that configures all aspects of existence in economic terms." (17) She joins Foucault in conceiving neoliberalism as "an order or normative reason" that becomes ascendant when it "takes shape as a governing rationality extending a specific formulation of economic values, practices and metrics to every dimension of human life." (30) This is not the same as claiming that neoliberalism literally marketizes all spheres of life, rather it points to how a neoliberal rationality *disseminates* the model of the market to an enlarged domain, one that reshapes subjects into financialised human capital. This includes a project to "self invest," in ways that enhance their value, to attract investors, across every sphere of existence, where, Brown continues, "all domains are markets, and we are everywhere assumed to be market actors." (36) In doing so, subjects become self-managed, subjugated, and docile, passively, consenting to this way of life.
94. As the Marxist economic geographer David Harvey explains, Hayek and the Mont Pelerin attendees "chose their topic wisely." Taking "human dignity" and "individual freedom" as fundamental—indeed as the central values of civilisation—is a "compelling and seductive" ideal (David Harvey, *A Brief History of Neoliberalism*, Oxford: Oxford University Press, 2004, 5) since these were the values that had been (and continued to be) threatened by dictatorships and communism, but also, as the attendees saw it, by all forms of state intervention that substituted collective judgements for individual choice. That individual choice included "the freedom of the consumer in choosing what he shall buy, the freedom of the producer in choosing what to make, and the freedom of the worker in choosing his occupation

foundations of "competitive order"—a society in which
an effectively competitive environment, the market,
is the main agency for the direction of activity.[95]

Last night, at home in Turin, I decide to ascertain
whether or not my mother has an emergency backpack
ready. My suspicion is that if she does, as she claims,
she's probably forgotten to pack it. Or there may be no
bag at all. It might be just an idea rather than a reality.
I phone her in Berkshire, where she has lived with my
Surrey-shaped, very English father for forty-eight years.
She picks up. In my mind she is in her bedroom, looking
into her Berkshire garden, which is not unlike a garden
you might find in Surrey.
　"Mum. Do you *really* have an emergency bag
ready?"
　"I do," she says, "but it needs more things."
　"So, what more would you need?"
　"Well, it's got all the basics and it's right here by the
side of the bed. In the wardrobe. It's always here. The
big stripy bag. You know, the one I take to the beach."
　"And this is your emergency bag?"
　"Yes. But it needs more things. This bag would only
work for English emergencies. For instance, it could do

and his place of employment." This amounts to the right
of each individual to "plan their own life" as they think best
in order to "maximise output in terms of individual satisfac-
tion." Such freedom, they held, can *only* be preserved when
"an effective competitive market is the main agency for all
economic activity." (Bruce Caldwell, *Mont Pèlerin 1947*,
165–166).
95. The attendees unanimously agreed that unless a government actively creates then maintains a climate for the competitive order, competition will not occur. Hence government activity should be reduced to an absolute minimum:
creating and maintaining an environment favourable
to competition, in which the free market can thrive,
and "freedom to choose" could flourish.

with a pair of sturdy shoes. So I can outrun a compromised building."

Actualities from the past are an environment. They condition and produce a series of clinical signals or anatomical signs in the nervous system. At the centre of that system—the nerve centre—is the present: the core of all our entanglements, a map of historical and social conditioning. Contrary to fantasies of colonising Mars, or solutions from the Centre for the Study of Existential Risk, most of us will remain on Earth for the foreseeable future. We are very preoccupied here, scrapping around in our environments trying to piece together the worry, fix the broken neurons, and understand, approximately, what happened.

My grandmother has been moving furniture since my mother or I can remember. Every weekend, we visit her home and things are very much altered: an extra sofa appears in the extension room, an armchair is relocated upstairs, indoor furniture is outside, the garden is dug up and remodelled, a tree is replanted, a bucket is filled with shoes, a rockery has been invented. A precisely organised living room, seen the week before in a stable and organised state, has been heavy-lifted, reconfigured with tools and power she musters from her 135-centimetre-tall force field. We surmise that the well-arranged scenography must have, at moments, been strewn about, exploded into heaps and piles of things, then reconfigured hurriedly before guests arrive. Taking things apart, then reassembling them differently, proves that things can always be otherwise, but how she assembles this proof, including the transportation of substantial pieces of bulky furniture up and down stairs, is a complete mystery. We assume she moves things at night.

In the years following the meeting at Mont Pèlerin, those thirty-nine liberals have the luck of the draw. Consumerism booms.[96] Apparently and understandably, no one wants to have their dresses lengthened and hemmed by their mum using spare bits of old cloth,

---

96. To persuade folks to *consent* to their vision, the Mont Pelerin attendees had to appeal to "common sense"— a hegemonic, shared ideology of the populous. By gathering around a single idea—freedom—an idea that ran deep enough to appear "common" and "intuitive" the attendees were on good tracks to succeed, yet, still, convincing the public about the "common sense" benefits of *market-enabled freedom* took some time. Through a major effort to evolve their ideology, they infiltrated popular culture and opinion with a strategy that emphasised the *freedom of consumer choice*. Choice extended from consumer products, to lifestyles, modes of expression, and a whole range of cultural practices and behaviours that would encourage individuals to metabolise "freedom." In the US, this began in 1971, by means of a confidential memo—sent by Lewis Powell (who was about to be elevated to the Supreme Court by Richard Nixon) to the US chamber of Commerce—arguing that criticism and opposition to US free enterprise had gone "too far" and a new strength was needed from the ingenuity and resources of American business. The National Chamber of Commerce, he argued, should lead an assault upon the major institutions—universities, schools, the media, publishing, the courts, to change how individuals think about "the corporation, the law, culture, and the individual" (memo is cited in Harvey, *A Brief History of Neoliberalism*, 43). The memo worked. A large cultural project was activated, infiltrating popular culture and consciousness with a philosophy of freedom, including former president of The Mont Pelerin Society, Milton Friedman, turning his book *Free to Choose* (co-authored with his wife, Rose) into a popular TV show. Video chapters from 1980 include: "The Power of the Market," "The Tyranny of Control," "Anatomy of Crisis," "What's Wrong with Our Schools? Who Protects the Consumer?," and "How to Stay Free." A 1990 edition of "The Power of the Market" came complete with an introduction narrated by Arnold Schwarzenegger.

or wash daily only the parts of their body—hands, forearms, legs, knees—that had gotten most dirty depending on age and profession. Many Westerners find something to spend their earnings on, exuberantly looking towards a future: Tupperwares, toys, electric hair dryers, bedroom bureaus, vacuum cleaners, canned peas in syrup, fish fingers, venetian blinds, Dunlopillo mattresses, and beyond arrive rapidly and "drive the past away."[97] Due partly to the creation of consumer behaviours, the Mont Pelerin vision of a very free-market-driven society becomes a success and a hegemony[98], and yet there are parts of society that "of course" must be kept out of this competitive order: "We must of course not forget that there are in a modern community a considerable number of services which are needed, such as sanitary and health services, and which could not possibly be provided by the market for the obvious reason that no price can be charged to the beneficiaries, or rather, that it is not possible to confine the benefits to those who are willing to pay for it," confirms von Hayek

---

97. References are from Annie Ernaux's *The Years* (New York: Penguin, 2008) and from my mum, who has a strong dislike of having her clothes made or adapted by Grandma, and is an exuberant purchaser of multiple Dyson vacuum cleaners and fish fingers.

98. Over half the men in the room would become twenty-two of the seventy-six economic advisors on Ronald Reagan's 1980s election campaign. Margaret Thatcher appointed Milton Friedman (chair of the Mont Pelerin Society), as her macroeconomic adviser. Thatcher also shows her indebtedness to the Mont Pelerin vision in an anecdote: not long after becoming Leader, visiting the Conservative Party's research department or party conferences (the myth is divided on which) then reaching into her briefcase, pulling out a copy of Hayek's early work, *The Constitution of Liberty*, and banging it on the table.

"*This*," she is said to have said while holding the 400-page book aloft, "is what we believe."

in his opening speech in 1947.[99] And yet the leaking
influence of markets can be oddly, unexpectedly,
and opaquely absorbed, metabolised by osmosis.[100]

99. Caldwell, *Mont Pèlerin 1947*.
100. The Mont Pelerin vision first infiltrated academia,
then public policy, spawning think tanks such as the
Institute of Economic Affairs in London (courtesy of Hayek)
and shaping the University of Chicago's economics program
(via Milton Friedman). There Friedman and his colleagues,
known as "the Chicago Boys," made international waves by
promoting "economic liberalism," including low taxes, the
sale of state-owned industries, the removal of protectionist
barriers, the primacy of private rather than government finance, and, philosophically, bolstering the individual above
the state. Yet, the first metabolization of Neoliberalism arrived, not in the Euro-American circuits that Hayek forged,
but rather, unexpectedly, in the periphery: in Chile. There,
neoliberalism landed abruptly, in the form of an "experiment" imposed by the dictator Augusto Pinochet, supported
by the Chicago Boys, who had been summoned by the US
government to help reconstruct the Chilean economy. This
relation did not arise from nowhere. The US had funded the
training of Chilean economists at the University of Chicago
since the 1950s—as part of a Cold War program to counter-
act left-wing tendencies in Latin America—and by the early
1970s, this training swung into the spotlight when business
elites mobilised this knowledge to organise opposition to the
socialist leader, Salvador Allende (a Keynesian) through a
sub-group known as the Monday Club. After Allende was
overthrown via a coup, Pinochet brought the Monday Club
and its economic policies firmly into his governmental fold.
Under Pinochet's watch, the Club negotiated loans with the
IMF, then restructured the economy according to their theories: they reversed the nationalisation and privatised public
assets, opened up natural resources (fisheries, timber, etc.)
to private and unregulated exploitation, privatised social
security, and facilitated a freer trade program. These swift
structural adjustments were harsh. They subjected Chile
to two major depressions in one decade, first in 1974–75,
when GDP fell by 12 per cent, then again in 1982–83, when
it dropped by 15 per cent. Thus, contrary to ideological ex-
pectations, a positive correlation between free markets and
robust growth cannot be proven in this first instance of neo-

Nonetheless, at this moment the British government establishes an important civic extension (the NHS) to their cradle-to-grave welfare program—an extension that will deplete later, due to a direction for society dreamed up at that same moment by thirty-nine individuals in Switzerland—and my grandmother and her Polish husband buy a house, with another Polish man and his Italian wife, in Surrey.

In this house of two Polish men and two talkative Italian women, my mother is born and is taught many things: how to lick her finger so as to thumb through newspaper pages very fast, how to spit with great accuracy, and, thanks to a 1958 edition of *The Book*

---

liberalism, nor in any example since. In Chile, the average GDP growth in 1974–89—the radical phase of the Pinochet revolution—was only 2.6 per cent. By comparison, during 1951–71—when the state held a more significant "planning" role, under Allende's socialist government—Chile's economy grew by an average of 4 per cent a year. (Stats from https://www.theguardian.com/global-development/ poverty-matters/2013/apr/16/legacy-margaret-thatcher-neoliberalism). This was—as David Harvey frames it—a test in the margins that became "a model for the formulation of policies in the center." (Harvey, *A Brief History of Neoliberalism*, 9) paving the way for Thatcherism and Reaganomics. What followed, in both the US and the UK, and indeed elsewhere including but not limited to India, Sweden, Australia, and (a more complicated story) China, was several decades of jostling about between the 1990s and 2010s shifts, tweaks, and cuts to the social agenda. By the time the conservative governments of Thatcher and Reagan had left office, those that followed (Bill Clinton, Barack Obama, Tony Blair) were all equally unable (and unwilling) to divert the resulting "no alternative" neoliberal fire-sale, culminating in a catastrophic new order: the introduction of tuition fees at universities; workfare in the place of welfare; austerity to "balance the books." This new world reared its head for all to see on September 15, 2008, when the 168-year-old investment bank Lehman Brothers, with $639 billion in assets, filed the largest bankruptcy in US history. It was bailed out by the US Federal Government.

of Knowledge volumes 1 through 8, sourced by my grandma, how to absorb facts. She teaches herself to read from bus stop signs and helps out in the house of double adults: filling out betting slips, corresponding with the Home Office, completing everyone's tax returns, and enrolling herself in secondary school.

In 1960 my grandparents manage to buy a house of their own. Some years later, they move on to the house I know, in which my Polish grandfather is a steady, matter-of-fact presence in a home of moving "Italian" parts. Elsewhere, in Surrey, Domenico still wears his luxury Italian clothes, by now deteriorated. He rides his motorbike at top speed through the English country-side, revving up the idyllic Surrey Hills, wearing half a leather football as a helmet. He moves to a council house with a wraparound garden—space enough to fabricate concrete "rococo" garden sculptures of cats, rabbits, terrazzo vases. He frescoes the carpet, paints the kitchen orange with white spots, plays his violin and his mandolin too loudly, annoys the camp adminis-trator, buys Alfa Romeos, takes them apart, puts the parts in different places, then buries a car in the garden.

One thing I have never understood but am trying to understand is this feeling that I must remain on high alert for something to go terribly, terribly wrong.
"Always have a bag ready," my mother tells me. Neither of us call this neurotic. She says it's empower-ing. I might call it a part of her extensive and powerful knowledge that death has always already arrived, and within this knowledge, many people have lived resil-iently, joyfully. I would also go so far as to say that it is part of her knowledge that you need to take care. The world is unpredictably dangerous.
Later, in Turin, I phone my mother back.
"Does Dad have an emergency beach bag?"

"Of course he doesn't!" she says. "He hasn't even thought about it."

My grandparents marry in 1954. My grandma is fifteen years younger than my Polish grandad. He's arrived in England in a roundabout way, after being held in "a hole in the ground, under a bit of tarpaulin," for two Russian winters, then rescued, rerouted, and invited to settle in the United Kingdom, but not granted citizenship.[101] From here on he works as a farm labourer, digs holes for the Surrey Electricity Board, reads electric metres, and does other odd jobs until he retires. While sofas move, chairs relocate, beds travel downstairs, and newly discovered old tablecloths are laid on freshly positioned tables, he cracks walnuts in his skinny bare hands, beats his grandchildren at arm wrestling and card games, digs his allotment, and watches boxing or the Australian soap opera *Neighbours*. A proper English retirement for a man of eighty who wants to remain as far away as possible, in actuality and culturally, from Stalin's brand of communism and, indeed, from any more holes in the ground.

In Grandma's kitchen, leftover food is conjured into multi-vegetable soups, odd omelettes, and mysteriously compiled meatballs, which she never once sits down to eat. Instead she sends food out in phases, to be passed around the always-hungry extended family, who are scattered throughout the house: perched on newly positioned wooden chairs, lounging on flower-patterned sheets tucked over bargain-hunted sofas, rummaging through bags of clothes or shop-bought broken biscuits.

---

101. During WWII, while he fights for the Polish Second Corps, he is imprisoned by the Soviet Army, who hold him in the hole. Then, via a Churchill-instigated prisoner swap, he is pulled out of the hole by the British, sent to North Africa to be trained to fight better, then transported to Tripoli to help win a strategic battle. For his efforts he is invited to settle in the UK.

In the downstairs bathroom, an event gains traction
week by week: shoes pile high into a tower, obstructing
any grandchild's access to the sink, demanding immense
resourcefulness from any small user in their handwashing.
The tallest men are rallied to help. My own somewhat
scientific English father (over six feet two, and thus particularly useful to Grandma) confirms he has shifted approximately *two tons* of soil for her creative "projects"
in the garden. Yet, if no help comes, she will manage.
Earth, objects, kilos of fabric, enormous pieces of furniture change location with velocity and amplitude.
As the story goes, one ordinary day Granddad climbs
upstairs to dress, then yells back down the staircase in
his thick Polish accent, "Marie! Where is wardrobe!?"

My grandmother does not know the cause of her mother's
death. She may have died from pneumonia, contracted
in March, while she tended goats in the coldness of early
spring. She may have died from something else, though.
To my mind, not knowing seems like a painful burden.
My mother—a pragmatic, well-trained historian—is
less forgiving of my guesswork and lazy, uninformed
emotions. "Look it up in the medical records in Reggio!"
she quips. Of course I haven't looked it up. My grandmother didn't look it up. The thought is so unlikely.
I imagine she didn't think to. I can relate. I imagine
she must have been in a spin, running around wartime
Reggio Calabria, a child, a small teenager, grieving,
busy, effervescent, bright and charming as ever.
    My grandma has knowledge of another mother's
death: her *grand*mother's. It is 1908. Beneath a collapsed
building, Domenico's mother is buried. He is five years
old. A 7.5 magnitude earthquake has struck Messina.
From under the rubble, Domenico hears his mother
praying out loud to the Virgin Mary, until she dies.
Domenico tells this story often to my grandma. I am
told he tells her using his fullest emotions, as is his way.

The tale implants in her immature consciousness for eternity.

When my grandma is born she has about two hundred billion brain cells, but for the most part, these are not wired together. In the first five years of her life, like any child's developing brain, my grandmother's brain cells connect up to create neural pathways after they are sent signals from her mother, her facilitating environment. A parent smiles at their baby. The baby smiles back. Brains develop. However a child is treated in the present one day becomes a child's past, and that past creeps into all its relationships in the future. We all reciprocate each other, all the time. Beliefs, behaviours, and patterns all are passed back and forth, mutually held, and become ingrained. This wiring of the brain is a writing that impacts personalities, relationships, parenting, communication, and worldviews. It has transgenerational ripples and effects that are social, psychological, and familial, possibly even genetic.[102] We can rewire our brains at any age, yet, this is challenging. Whatever gets laid down at the start sticks hard. This makes it clear to me that my grandma's mother—her holding environment, though temporary—was more than good enough.

By the 1990s, five grandchildren are rampaging over a Polish/Italian landscape, diving into heaps of hoarded clothes that fit no one. In this massive jumble, a desire for earthly clutter pings around the room and we wear everything: off-cuts of sheep skins discarded from the jackets of wealthy men in Reigate whom my grandma tailors clothes for, nets from wedding dresses she's working on, patterned bedsheets from the market,

---

102. Echo Online, "Class 3: Child Development," *Trauma-Informed Nonviolent Parenting Classes*, https://echotraining. talentlms.com/catalog/info/id:133.

a tea cosy shaped like a chicken, which we take
turns wearing as a hat. As we rummage, grandma
goes about her business. Half very deliberately
dressed, half accidentally dressed, this is her look:
part shaman, part child, part power-dresser. She is
standing on her toes to reach the hob, stirring a soup,
poking about in the oven, shaking irregularly chopped
potato chips, shutting the oven with a foot or an
elbow, leaving trays of chicken breasts crackling behind the baked glass of the door. Elsewhere we raid
a bedroom bureau installed at that moment downstairs, and find handfuls of everything: ancient family
photos, packs of Parma Violets, earrings, balls of
wool, balls for sport—any of the above are equipment
for grandma to play throw-and-catch with, to display
her dexterity. She is explaining why she is very clever
and *very* strong to anyone who is trying to watch
the television. She is dribbling a basketball, she is
under someone's arm, pulling up her skirts, showing
her magnificent suntanned legs, squishy knees, holding
a grandchild, who—no matter its newborn weight
or length—appears enormous when carried
by Grandma.

While she is busy with these matters, stuffed photo
albums are opened, and the contents fall out. We rifle
through the spillage of postcards, electricity bills, sepia
images of babies sitting in buckets, Polish men in hats
and suits, squinting in the sun, trouser legs rolled up.
In the garden, we ponder Domenico's rococo sculptures, impressed by the calcified cat, the white plaster
rabbit, several corniced vessels, now planted rakishly
by Grandma in her DIY raised flower beds alongside
a taverna chair or two. We poke about in the greenhouse, discover a stash of high-heeled shoes, pull out
bags within bags, stuff within stuff. We travel indoors
to loot drawers of rosaries, purses, buttons, gold-ish
rings. While Grandma hybridises us into one long

name jumble, so that where one grandchild begins and the next ends becomes irrelevant, likewise her children. We all admire a soft toy monkey and a plastic motorised bull, displayed proudly on a kitchen shelf with the plates. A wardrobe, tightly packed, might readily burst open and collapse on top of us, it felt, yet on the surface, all rooms are immaculately arranged and stable. My grandma keeps the house really nicely. She likes to have a clean sight line.

In *The Writing of the Disaster* (1980), Maurice Blanchot tells us that "in the work of mourning, it is not grief that works: grief keeps watch."[103] Grief is an unmeasurable vigil, not a constant vigilance. Grief means spending time with the conditions and one another without any objective or end point. Grandma's life has lost things of greater or lesser importance along the way: front-door keys, clothing, large pieces of furniture, and empty bags within empty bags. Thanks to disorder, the thing you might be missing, maybe the thing you are grieving, might show up underneath the piles of stuff perhaps years, maybe decades, or maybe a lifetime later, revealed by a new arrangement. Everything is allowed to go missing so that everything can be found, recovered, with "a roar of cosmic energy."[104]

In 1999, my grandma turns seventy. She buys a tiny second home in Spain with cash savings. She is infinitely southern Italian. She needs the sun. Travelling to Italy is too expensive. Mass tourism means reaching the Costa Blanca is economical and easy. She walks to the Thomas

---

103. Maurice Blanchot, *The Writing of the Disaster* (Lincoln: University of Nebraska Press, 1995), 51.
104. Rosi Braidotti, "Writing as a Nomadic Subject," *Comparative Critical Studies* 11, no. 2/3 (2014): 172, https://rosibraidotti.com/wp-content/uploads/2018/06/Braidotti-Rosi-Writing-as-a-Nomadic-Subject.pdf.

Cook travel shop regularly, and chats nonstop in her heavy Italian accent with travel agents she has charmed. They find her good tickets. On the flights to and from Spain she never checks luggage. She carries one of her many odd handbags on board. On her return, she is always fantastically tanned, wearing shorts and perhaps an oversized "Come to Alicante" T-shirt with a glittery dolphin on it, like an excited 135-centimetre-tall child. Her carry-on bag, still unpacked, is at the foot of the stairs. Rifling through it, as we always do with all her things, I find a bag within that bag, a sequined purse, a £20 note, and—more than once—an uncooked potato.

My grandma's desire to live is a desire that is in and of the Earth. It does not transcend the Earth, aside from her southern Italian *need* to go to heaven (but that is a more complicated story, for another time). Her desires —manifesting in her many acts of heavy lifting, in each new arrangement she makes—belong to the foundations of everything that *endures* and *exists*. These are desires that come before Hollywood directs our future/fictional selves, before Jane Austen makes a husband or a wife the ultimate covetable thing, before Madame Bovary reads fashion magazines and desires to be someone else, before Sigmund Freud sexes everything. These are desires found before the nineteenth or the eighteenth century, all the way back to Baruch Spinoza,[105] who, says Gilles Deleuze, "is not one of those who think that a sad passion has something good about it."[106]

---

105. The examples, except Madame Bovary, come from Rosi Braidotti, who spoke of them at her summer school, *Posthuman Ethics, Pain, and Endurance (How to Live an Anti-Fascist Life and Endure the Pain)*, August 20–24, 2018, Utrecht.
106. "There is, then, a philosophy of 'life' in Spinoza; it consists precisely in denouncing all that separates us from life, all these transcendent values that are turned against life.

Hers is a desire to take in the world with all its negativity, problems, or sadness and respond with an outpouring of joy. Any god, any belief, is way more vocal and manifest in those piles of clothes, in the concrete cats and pots, in her reorganisation of the cracks in which she remains entirely buried in history.

Once, my grandmother tells my mother that she wonders if her own mother died from worry. To this, my pragmatic mother replies, "Impossible nonsense. What could she have been worried about?" My grandma is wary of catching a cold in March. She is worried about Naples being dangerous. She is worried that I moved to Italy. My mother is not worried about being unprepared. She has her bag packed. She never wants to live where her maternal-grandmother lived, because she is very pragmatic. Plus, she tells me, "March is the deadly month in Italy." Or maybe Italy reminds her of earthquakes, Messina, her grandfather, his tales of a great-grandmother she never met, and this makes her worry. I'm always worried, waiting for something to go terribly wrong, without reason. I moved to Italy, maybe because there was a circuit to close. Now I am an Italian citizen and I feel a little less worried, possibly because the United Kingdom is several thousand miles removed. Some things appear to have no reason and no answers. Time does not flow in one direction. Some situations do not settle.

…Spinoza traces, step by step, the dreadful concatenation of sad passions; first, sadness itself, then hatred, aversion, mockery, fear, despair, *morus conscientiae*, pity, indignation, envy, humility, repentance, self-abasement, shame, regret, anger, vengeance, cruelty." Gilles Deleuze, *Spinoza: Practical Philosophy*, trans. Robert Hurley (San Francisco: City Lights Books, 1998), 26.

"Take it!" grandma says when I say I like her necklace. "Take it!" she says when I leave for the airport and she waves a twenty-pound note at me. "Take them!" she says, kicking off her size-three shoes, handing me her big skirts, or her blazers, or her knitted pillows. "Take it!" she says to Franca, my three-and-a-half-year-old daughter, when Franca appreciates my grandma's much-needed, tiny walking stick. Franca keeps the stick, delighted. Grandma says she will open a shop, she has always said so. That's why she has so many clothes, that is what she will do. She is talking nonstop about the future, what she will do next, what she can improve, what she can move, where she will move to, what she will do in ten years' time, what she will do when she is 120, when she will go back to her tiny house in Spain. But even while her head is in the future, somehow reluctant to settle[107], I find her exceptionally present.

107. Liveness is a refusal to settle. This refusal has a different status to the relentless productivity and surplus activity so integral to the performance principle. Rather, it is closer to Gertrude Stein's "continuous present"; staying with the same material, handling it again then again, saying the same thing, differently. Maintaining and caring for ongoing material means turning it over with curiosity, while willingly changing, moving, adjusting that matter in minor ways. Understanding how to propel, take flight, by means of life drives (eros) and instincts, sociality, collision, is as much a knowledge, as anything else. Liveness moves in more than one direction at once, not only back and forth. It moves vibrantly, erratically, because it does so within limits. It moves democratically, since it needs to be constantly revisited, in order to thrive, in a state of infinite rehearsal. Liveness is a voice, a means—a method—from the intersectional struggles experienced by women who—to tell stories—have needed to steer away from male constructions, including the third person, the gaze, the novel, and the ego—to invent new genres and languages that might better handle and hold embodied knowledge: untellable, ongoing stories—restlessness, refusals to settle.

Recently, travelling to Switzerland on a work trip, I am on the plane, and I open my handbag. I am surprised to find an uncooked sweet potato inside.

In July 2019, our twins are born, my milk comes in, and I have a sweaty hormonal hallucination.[108] It runs like this: I am sitting on top of a mountain of clothes talking with three women. Suddenly I remember: I have a newly born baby. She is buried beneath the clothes I am sitting on. I hurriedly pull the fabric apart, plunge my arms into the pile, and pull out my tiny daughter. She is filthy, covered in mud. She is also absolutely fine. This scenario continues to give me a strong sense of assurance that things are going okay.

In 2021, in the middle of a COVID-19 winter, my grandma stops moving furniture. From Torino, I listen to the details relayed by my mother over the phone.

"She is not swallowing and she appears to be hallucinating, she is vacant, but the doctors say it doesn't seem like a stroke."

"She's had a breakdown." I say. "Of course she has. She needs to talk to someone." But that is a very long story. Too long for the NHS to track and trace and rewire. And besides, tests show bacterial bronchitis. So that is that, sort of.

Folktales and fables are often filled with missing mothers. Every century is full of such tales. They begin in individuals, but they are taken on and worn by others. Too many origins, not enough time, too many stories to heal. My grandmother's children respond, typically exuberant and canny. They find ways to visit the hospital

---

108. I know: dull to talk about such things. No one wants to hear another person's dreams. Bad etiquette. But here it is all the same.

ward despite COVID-19 rules. They keep her going, take her food, bring her back to life, get her brain scanned, take her home. Now my mum, her sister, and her brother are at their mother's house all the time, in the home of moving parts, keeping an eye on grand-ma when she wakes at three in the morning and worries and prepares to move furniture.

While she distractedly looks for her mother, who's hobbled off somewhere, I ask my mother over the phone: "Do you have generational trauma?" "Oh, probably," she replies, preoccupied. "Most people do, but what can you do?" I tell her the symptoms might include (in individuals or communities) hypervigilance, a sense of shortness of life, a sense of a short future, mistrust, aloofness, high anxiety, nightmares, a very sensitive fight-or-flight response. She tells me she has her bag packed. I tell her that without a synthesis of his-tories, situations, and grief, traumatised individuals or communities might fly into bad reactions, bad passions, emergency mode, cut themselves off like a shell company. There are many ways an individual or a society might *respond* to the generational terror of never knowing what's going to happen: consult an oracle, check some data, buy a bunker in New Zealand, fly to Mars, *react* with a relentlessly competitive order to rank, rate, measure, manage, marketize, and perform everything. All of which might promise to take away the fear, and the pain, of not knowing. Or they might move a lot of furniture. She knows, she says. She has her beach bag ready. But now she needs to go find Grandma.

Pull out a bureau drawer, look in the greenhouse, fling open a cupboard, sift through a bucket of shoes; you never know what you might find. You never know when you might need a £20 note, a necklace, a tea cosy, a mandolin, half a leather football. You never know

when you might leave, or if you might return, when
you might need your bag-within-a-bag, when you
might need a potato to make soup, when an environment might hold you, or be unable to hold you.
Everything and anything elicits reactions.

Maybe too much is assumed, though, at that preliminary meeting in 1947 in Switzerland.

The competitive order is an environment—one
particular response to a recent, war-damaged past,
propelled from a grieving and understandably future-
hungry global population. This response is created,
and shaped. Yet comprehensive considerations of what
should not become a competitive order and what a government *must provide outside the market* do not appear
to be typed up in the 1947 meeting transcripts that
were notated so diligently by von Hayek's secretary.[109]
As decades passed, the Mont Pelerin vision would
morph into neoliberalism: first tested in Chile, next in
Reaganomics in America, and then in Thatcher's
Britain, where many things that were neither imagined
nor intended for the marketplace became markets.

The present is my grandma's home. This is a nerve centre.
The core of social, historical entanglements in which
a ninety-four-year-old stays awake, holds vigil, holds
power. Holding vigil takes practice. Which is to say:
holding vigil takes myths, histories, ideas, languages,
various bits of moving furniture, a surprising pagan

---

109. The topic of eliminating poverty takes up seven pages,
in over two hundred pages of meeting transcripts. There
is just one mentioning of social resources and services,
yet this consideration is neither ring-fenced, nor discussed.
Firm limits on what should never be sent to market were
not drawn up, because firm boundaries—limits of any kind
—would not and never could be, in their eyes, freedom.
Eighty years later, we are living in this neglectful omission.

spirit that does not extinguish, a mind that does not contract or extract. One hundred thirty-five centimetres tall, wildly ignorant of competitive orders, and miraculously buoyant—this is a hero to me, an environment worthy of serious attention.

A HYPOTHESIS OF RESISTANCE

CHAPTER 4

This is an essay on

UNDETECTABILITY

Though less like an essay, and more like a ecology.
Parts may or may not sync up, we will see.

It's 1991. A primary lateral incisor from the lower jaw
is creamy white with a jagged edge. Between the slightly
yellowed root is a crevice, blackened with old blood.
The incisor is in a palm-size box, square and sturdy, em-
bellished with a golden pattern. It was probably picked
up by my mother in Brighton, or at the WOMAD festi-
val. A red ribbon attaches the lid to the base, and inside
that base is a hollow. In the hollow is a red satin lining,
and on top of the satin is this child's tooth.

It's spring. Six days after the end of the Second World
War. After years of living under Fascism, localities with
a long tradition of local initiative have taken matters
into their own hands. In a small village a few miles
from the town of Reggio Emilia in northern Italy,
a woman is salvaging and washing pieces of brick.
Having heard a rumour, the pedagogue and psychiatrist
Loris Malaguzzi jumps on his bike and rides over to see
with his own eyes. Indeed, it is true: the villagers
are building a school.[110]

---

110. Lella Gandini, "History, Ideas and Basic Principles:
An Interview with Loris Malaguzzi," in *The Hundred
Languages of Children: The Reggio Emilia Approach
to Early Childhood Education*, ed. Carolyn Edwards,
Lella Gandini, and George Forman (New York:
Ablex, 1993), 42.

It's the sixth century CE. Following the orders of the
Roman Emperor Justinian, monks are hiding *Bombyx
mori*—silkworm eggs—in the hollows of some reeds.
They smuggle these from China into the Byzantine
Empire, thus introducing silk production to the West.
Much later, between the eighth and the ninth centuries,
on the initiative of Arab or Byzantine immigrants, south-
ern Italy becomes an epicentre of the silk industry.[111]

It's March 15, 1666, and the king of France, Louis XIV,
takes his first military review of eighteen thousand men.
The king conducts a military exercise with a stick. To
his left, several ranks show soldiers' full faces perfectly
aligned. They raise their right arms to shoulder height
and hold their rifles strictly vertically; their right legs
are slightly forward, their left feet are turned outward.
On the ground, lines intersect at right angles beneath
the shoulders—wide rectangles that serve as references
for different phases in the exercise's positions, "frozen
into a uniformly repeated attitude of ranks and lines."[112]

Before the age of six, by which time a child in Italy
must attend school, whether or not their parents work,
the child will need somewhere to go during the day.
Ideally this place, external to the home, will regard
and respond as the child moves through complex
processes: say, presenting itself in the dramatic role
of newly born penguin taking its first wobbling steps,
then cooking with stones that hatch into baby penguins,
then feeding and sustaining a soft toy penguin with
grapes and a bottle of *acqua frizzante*, then building
a long-term project around their interest in polar birds.

111. Stefano Comino and Alessandro Gasparetto, "Silk
Mills in Early Modern Italy," *Advances in Historical Studies*
9, no. 5 (December 2020): https://www.scirp.org/journal/
paperinformation.aspx?paperid=104670.
112. Foucault, *Discipline and Punish*, 188.

"That looks very good," Grand Duke Mikhail remarked when he inspected a regiment that presented their arms for over an hour. Yet, "only… " one small problem. "They breathe."[113]

Before a child's permanent incisor pokes through its gum, the child's thinking is intuitive. Around the age that they cut this second set of teeth, the child is considered "ready" to leave the world of symbolic representation and apply themselves to complex concepts—cause and effect, time, calculation. "Readiness" marks the shift from what Jean Piaget, a Swiss psychologist known for his work on child development, calls the "intuitive" preoperational stage (age three to six) to the concrete operational stage (age seven to eleven), when the child can engage with arithmetic, reading, and writing without becoming exhausted and confused.

Having been handled with so much curiosity by me and my brother, I think the tooth went missing.

113. *Ibid.* This reference arrives just after Foucault has discussed King Louis XIV's tightly regimented, first military review of eighteen thousand men in 1666. Within the same page Foucault jumps three hundred years, and across several national borders, to recount the anecdote of a "Grand Duke Mikhail," mentioned in *Memoirs of A Revolutionist* by former Russian aristocrat turned anarchist, Peter Kropotkin. "Grand Duke Mikhail" seems likely to be the fourth child, and third son, of the Tsarevich Alexander Alexandrovich, born in St Petersburg in 1878. The Tsarist (1600–1800) regime of the time is fiercely disciplinary; and fierce discipline is a constructed behaviour. Even the most wild soldiers, and the most wild divisions—such as those controlled by Grand Duke Mikhail—can be streamlined and controlled into a tightly disciplined, machinic fighting force, one that will never commit mutiny. But do have to breathe.

Lately, our twins are coming home from their new municipal preschool covered in mud. Their second teeth have not yet come through, so someone else is taking care of their intuitive space. At nine in the morning they take the bus on their own to one of the hills just beyond the city centre. They spend the day mainly outside. They come home at half past three clutching sticks and drawings, emboldened by their daily achievements, about which they proudly tell us nothing when we ask, "So, what did you do today?" Instead, they turn their energies to laser-focused displays of knot tying and polar bird impersonations.

In the twelfth and thirteenth centuries, silk twisting is performed manually, with the use of spinning wheels. With this technique, only one thread at a time can be processed, keeping operations considerably slow. Progress is later made thanks to the hand-wound mechanical silk mill, employed for the first time in Italy in Lucca in the thirteenth century. Several silk threads can be twisted simultaneously, and the quality of the resulting yarn is "perfectly homogeneous." This technology might be understood as the first factory.[114]

As mills increased in size, they required the use of more powerful energy sources. Hydraulically driven mills developed, contributing to the phenomenon of mass production and subsequently providing a useful symbolic representation from which many of the major male heavyweights of nineteenth- and twentieth-century continental philosophy would draw their conclusions.

It's 1974. At Sussex University—a hotbed of social reform, protests, new social policies, child development

---

114. Comino and Gasparetto, "Silk Mills in Early Modern Italy."

theories, and progressive pedagogy—my mother learns how to teach. Her approach to lesson planning has always been confidently open and responsive. "A child might walk to school, see a dead bird by the side of the road on the way, pick it up, take it to my classroom, and that would be the lesson for the day!" she tells me excitedly.

Conventionally, it's assumed that seventy-two months of age is enough time for a child to have reached a level of operational "readiness." Besides counting time, there are other ways of detecting readiness: a slightly smaller head, a slimmer torso, the appearance of arches in the feet, or an incisor poking through a gum.

By 1993 in the UK, the culture of child development theories, progressive pedagogy, emergent curriculum creation, and teacher agency is inspected and redefined by cultures of performance: visible output, measurability.

In 1956, driven by Karl Marx's precise observations of Manchester's factory regimes and Friedrich Engels's 1845 *The Condition of the Working Class in England*, Herbert Marcuse critically read Marxist studies through a rereading of Sigmund Freud.[115] He concluded that the inputs and outputs of hydraulically or coal driven factories, powered by the desires of the industrialists, repressed the worker's childlike eros—an intuitive, pleasure-driven "life instinct"—since this instinct

---

115. Besides being a study of labour, and indeed, Marxism —as its full title suggests—Marcuse's *Eros and Civilization* is also a singular *psychoanalytical* study, focusing not only on the condition of contemporary labour, but equally on the desires and repressed desires (and psychological possibilities) of labouring subjects. Indeed the book itself emerged after Marcuse was invited to give a series of lectures, in 1950–51, by the Washington School of Psychiatry.

in the factory is brought under codification and control of adult performance/reality principles: productiveness, toil, security, comparisons.[116]

In the late 1800s, with the need for labour at an all-time high, industrialists in Italy set up crèches in their factories for breastfed or newly weaned infants of working mothers. In Pinerolo, the silk mill's hydraulic engine rocked infants to sleep in their cradles.[117]

Today, from the preschool on the hill, communication with parents is kept to a minimum. I assume this is so that teachers can focus on confirming that the very slow, awkward walk of a particular three-and-a-half-year-old is 100 percent penguin.

"Ideally," my mother told me often while looking at the blood stained into the tooth's roots, "one would learn to read after the age of seven."

In 1925, after the unification of Italy, daycare centres—like the cradles at Pinerolo—contributed to the well-being and evolution of the National Agency for Maternity and Childhood (Opera nazionale per la protezione della maternità e dell'infanzia, ONMI).[118]

---

116. This diminishes eros, an energy of desire which could move through a subject, and power their sociopolitical imagination. Yet, in a performance society, the social imagination is diffused, repressively desublimated, because there is no surplus energetic flow left for eros. All surplus energy goes towards "the performance," flattening subjects into docility, so that they no longer live their own lives and take pleasure, they perform the dictates of their pre-established function. Subjects are thus dictated *to*, and their primitive, basic needs and instincts are reshaped by the preset inputs and outputs of their workplace. Today, desire is nudged and shaped by the unregulated environment of, say, Silicon Valley's platforms.
117. Edwards, Gandini, and Forman, "Introduction" in *The Hundred Languages of Children*, 13.
118. *Ibid.*

This helped establish early infant daycare—the *asilo nido* and the *scuola dell'infanzia*, supporting children before they reached school age.

The Fascist regime that took over Italy in 1922 took upon itself all the merits of the ONMI, yet adjusted them to adopt a medical-hygienic model of child care that was the prevailing trend of the time. It subsequently focused on one particular educational method, in which a close and special connection between a mother and her child would be re-created in a classroom set up to look and feel like a home. This naturalised, domestic approach was also favoured by the Catholic Church, as it produced a child in the image of how the Church understood children.

As Fascism evolved, it came to view women's reproductive work as a form of labour analogous to factory work, textile production, or automotive manufacturing. Children became industrial products and symbols of service to the nation.[119]

A quick Google search for "Madonna and Child" makes me feel so *mad*.

Having sold an abandoned war tank, a few trucks, and some horses left behind by the retreating Germans, the villagers in Reggio Emilia collectively raise funds for the construction of this first of many alternative schools. Loris Malaguzzi, the critical pedagogue, gets off his bike and asks: How will they finance this school project beyond its construction? Where are the teachers?[120]

"The rest will come," the villagers tell Malaguzzi, assuredly, as they work steadily and self-organizedly towards building a school in which children will teach

---

119. Matthew Wills, "Mussolini's Motherhood Factories," *JSTOR Daily*, April 1, 2022, https://daily.jstor.org/mussolinis-motherhood-factories/.
120. Loris Malaguzzi in Gandini, "History, Ideas and Basic Principles," 42.

one another and be taught by their environment as much as by teachers. And in which teachers learn what to teach—via a curriculum that is not set in advance, but which *emerges*—in response to the children, via the children's responses to external worlds, which the children are introduced to by their teachers.[121]

In his 2014 study *Signs and Machines*, Maurizio Lazzarato borrows a helpful term from Gilles Deleuze, which Deleuze had borrowed from psychoanalysis: "the *crushing* of enunciation." Such crushing is not suffered negatively. It is rarely experienced as repression. More typically it is experienced positively as an encouragement to "speak up," to communicate often, constantly, even, only for meaning to be crushed by the code that belongs to the apparatus—the analysis, the institution, the curriculum, the technology— through which one is trying to speak.[122]

> Try as one might, 'the entire interpretive and subjectivation machine exists to suppress the conditions of real expression.'[123]

The lips, tongue, hands, guts, scent, face, teeth—cut off from enunciation—give up on what was meant to be said.

---

121. *Ibid.*, 102.

122. On February 17, 2024, at 2.30 p.m.,in *A Thesis on Spillage*, Graham Foundation, Chicago, artist Tony Cokes reflected upon the production of subjects under capital. "We open up our smartphones, essentially to be commanded. . . this is a weight on our nervous system that wasn't previously there." He emphasises, via Deleuze: "communication is a command."

123. Maurizio Lazzarato, *Signs and Machines: Capitalism and the Production of Subjectivity* (Los Angeles: Semiotext(e), 2014), 164, quoting Michel Foucault, *The Courage of the Truth*, trans. Graham Burchell (New York: Palgrave Macmillan, 2011), 314.

Supported by Malaguzzi, the pedagogue, the Reggio method spread and influenced Europe as a progressive early-years educational program focused on long-term, engaging projects—communal activities—to open up topics for speculation and discussion. The method operates by supporting the hundreds of languages through which a child communicates, a communication through which their *intellect* emerges. A small selection of those languages here: singing, balancing, stick handling, digging, dancing, jumping, den construction, knot tying, painting, pretending to be a bird.

My mother proudly says that she can never remember her dreams, yet one of my earliest memories is her telling me about a recurring nightmare in which she would sit down to take an examination and all her teeth would come tumbling out. She had this nightmare in the 1990s, so, I guess, long after her teacher training exams at Sussex University.

As Marcuse tells it, the enclosure and the temporality of the factory migrate into the bodies and the unconscious minds of its workers. The worker is compulsively oriented to (and saturated with) the industrial codes of the factory's performance principles: accountability, output, measurability. Workers are codified in advance by their function. In *Signs and Machines*, Lazzarato searches for an example of more or less this. He names it "the performative"[124]: an utterance that is both

---

124. Performance is often spoken of alongside "performativity," a term indebted to J. L. Austin and Judith Butler. For Austin performativity manifests as a speech act in public, one that, in its utterance, creates a reality. A simple example is "I pronounce you man and wife", which, when uttered in the context of a wedding ceremony creates a new reality: husbands, wives, a marriage.

machinic and fleshy, and which *crushes* a subject with preexisting code via social and machinic forces. To explain the effects of "the performative," he holds up its opposite: the political rupture initiated when someone rises, bodily, in an assembly to "tell the truth" (*dire vrai*) in an act of parrhesia.[125]

Digging out this counter-example from Foucault's 1982–83 lectures, *The Government of Self and Others* —in which he presents parrhesia as a "rupture with the dominant significations," an "irruptive event" that creates a "fracture" and thus opens a situation up to effects that are, precisely, "not known"—Lazzarato notes that, inversely, the conditions and the effects of the "performative" enunciation are "codified" in advance. Thus, he continues, "the performative" represents a "form of enunciation" that is exactly the opposite of parrhesia.

Parrhesia is an utterance that transforms the dynamics of power, and thereby transforms both speakers and listeners.[126] Conversely, within Lazzarato's particular genre of the "performative," no such transformation is possible.

In Butler's *Gender Trouble: Feminism and the Subversion of Identity* (1990), performativity arrives when we act, speak, and talk in ways that create and consolidate the impression of a particular gender. The empowering potential of performativity is that we can act, utter and thus create a gender of our choosing. More recently, Maurizio Lazzarato, in *Signs and Machines: Capitalism and the Production of Subjectivity* (2014) shapes a theory of enunciation, language and subjugation that he terms "performative" yet which differs from the "performativity" theorised by Butler. He holds "a performative" to be a subjugating, machinic utterance through which a subject enunciates as an extension of the function inscribed in them by 'machines': say, a platform, a media, marketing, or a sovereign power.

125. *Ibid.*, 173
126. *Ibid.*, 173

The irruption of permanent teeth is a visible, tangible sign that a child is approaching a new age of thought. This is physical acknowledgment that a body is solidifying, and that its motoric and esoteric capacities are strengthening: quietly knotting adult belts, tying pine cones to the backs of chairs and leaving them there, taking care of five imaginary baby chicks, brown and yellow, newly hatched, then wearing adult sandals, ten sizes too large, to take the chicks for a swim without water outside on the balcony. Such focus demands a great deal of energy.

Energy is directed away from such activities by enamel pushing through hard tissue—the gingiva of the upper or lower jaws. This takes maximum esoteric energy, and weakens the body.

When Gilles Deleuze, Félix Guattari, and Michel Foucault wrote about Fascism, the dictatorships they spoke of were still partly in place across Europe. In the early 1970s, Portugal was still Fascist (until 1974), as were Spain (until 1975) and Greece (until 1974).

Today, writes Paul B. Preciado,

> fascism advances like a political corpse stubbornly taking the last steps before falling. Sometimes the dead assumes the form of a naked white guy with antlers on top of the head, other times an Italian businesswoman, or a national-security neocon-feminist mummy; sometimes it speaks English, sometimes Russian, but always the abstract language of the market.[127]

Fascism can be defined by its history: anti-intellectualism, the leader's cult, too violent, where justification is contained in the very state of affairs, a state that remains hegemonic, relentless. This is familiar, but

---

127. Paul B. Preciado, "I Am Falling in Love," *Artforum*, October 6, 2022, https://www.artforum.com/slant/i-am-falling-in-love-89412.

if we expect fascism today to look like Fascism looked in the 1940s or the 1970s, we will miss it.[128]

In the singular pursuit of meeting the competitive order within "personal" markets, individual performance becomes relentless. It seeps a principle of compulsory visibility and discipline into and onto that individual body, saturated with a particularly banal yet vicious, performative toxin: ranking.

As Foucault maps it out, a science of visual inspections, of endlessly repeated movements, resonates as an inherited, learned behaviour. It was perfected by the Napoleonic army, who learned it first from lycée schools that trained "the elite of the nation." The army honed the training, then handed schools back their evolution of inspections, with added tactical knowledge acquired during the Napoleonic wars. With this method, Western European schools (of the classical age) became an apparatus of uninterrupted examination. In doing so, education became less about "jousts in which pupils pitch their forces against one another" and increasingly "a perpetual comparison of each and all."[129]

From the 1990s onwards, schools in the UK's homogeneous delivery of the national curriculum would be *detected*, inspected, recorded, reported, then demoted to "inadequate" by the British government if underperforming.[130] Education became an industrial complex,

---

128. This phrase was buried in notes I took while Rosi Braidotti spoke, in person, on fascism, during the summer school she led and which I attended, *Posthuman Ethics, Pain, and Endurance (How to Live an Anti-Fascist Life and Endure the Pain)* [see footnote 105].
129. Foucault, *Discipline and Punish*, 186.
130. Xello UK team, "Ofsted Ratings," Xello (blog), October 11, 2022, https://cascaid.co.uk/ofsted-inspection-

leaching tactics and strategy from factory surveillance
and market codification into spaces for education.

Outstanding, Good, Requires Improvement,
Inadequate. "With the performative, there is no
invention or transformation of the subject possible."[131]

Outstanding, Good, Requires Improvement,
Inadequate. A preexisting code to communicate
turns a subject's utterance codified, speechless.[132]

At its most extreme—but also at its most domestic
and micro—almost every aspect of life can potentially
be made in the image of a market. The competitive
order (desired by the liberal elite for the past eighty
years) has succeeded. Individuals are codified: ranked
and visualised on a variety of trading screens, motored
by a new power paradigm that remains invisible at its
source, yet produces tangible symptoms elsewhere.

Absorbed and metabolised, performance moves
with us. This transference—from environment to
individuals—fires a mass automatic physiological
reaction in our shared, woven nervous system: stiffness
in the hips, reduced circulation in the legs, locking in
the lower back, constant communication, an unwillingness to move, wakeful sleep, ground-down molars.

---

framework/ratings/#:~:text=grade%201%3A%20outstand-
ing,grade%204%3A%20inadequate.

131. Lazzarato, *Signs and Machines*, 174.

132. Since I cannot be 100 per cent certain of the accuracy
of my transcription, as I hurriedly notated Rosi Braidotti's
off-script, enigmatic, and cartographic lectures, during her
summer school *Posthuman Ethics, Pain, and Endurance
(How to Live an Anti-Fascist Life and Endure the Pain)* [see
footnote 105]—I will leave this trace of her, the school, and
its ethos, for these footnotes: "Where is the curriculum in
your life!?" she asks us vividly while she gesticulates all
around her. We are open-mouthed, astonished by how this
philosopher speaks, her way of practising theory, in the flesh
and in the voice. "Find the curriculum!!!!!!" She enunciates
from the lectern, with humour and urgency. "And *kill it*!!!"

Dreaming of your teeth falling out is the most common of all adult nightmares. It's an anxiety dream, an under-performance dream. An oppression stirs. It's our sub-consciousness saying: we failed to communicate, truly.

A HYPOTHESIS OF RESISTANCE

CHAPTER 5

This is an essay on

DURATION

Perhaps less like an essay, more like a spillage.
Parts may or may not sync up, we will see.

My son is grabbing my throat, pushing his hands into
my neck, and shoving his fists in my armpits. Irritated,
I peel him off, plunk him on the floor, and walk away
coldly as a means of preventing such behaviour in the
future. He follows, calling out happily. His twin sister
has been watching, and trots after us, brightly telling
me: "Oh, you two have both been playing soooo
nicely!"

Disciplining the body has been one of the core precon-
ditions for capitalist development. In Silvia Federici's
view, such discipline proceeded slowly throughout the
seventeenth century and into the eighteenth, as the state
and the church transformed an individual's power into
labour power. In the nineteenth century, the naturalised,
normalised worker we know today was created:
> temperate, prudent, responsible, proud to possess
> a watch, and capable of looking upon the imposed
> conditions of the capitalist mode of production
> as 'self-evident laws of nature.'[133]

---

133. Silvia Federici, "Capitalism and the Sexual Division
of Labor," *Caliban and the Witch: Women, the Body and
Primitive Accumulation* (New York: Autonomedia, 2004),
https://theanarchistlibrary.org/library/silvia-federici-caliban-
and-the-witch. She attributes the first part of the quote to
E. P. Thomson and the second part to Karl Marx.

Reflecting on his undisciplined armpit poking and throttle attack, plus my daughter's naming this "playing," I realise my son's move is a tickle, because rather than investing in the demands of playing, I've been tickling *him*. Tickling a four-year-old is easier than playing with a four-year-old. Handling a state of spontaneity takes all of one's body knowledge. And I am very busy, writing this—temperate, prudent, eye on the clock—so it's easier to respond to him with a speedy jab to his stomach. But now this heavy-handed shortcut boomerangs back, grabs me by the neck, leaves me and my exterior irritated: wishing he would "behave less."

"Imagine what it would be like if you've never been told no."[134]

"Ahhhhh!" the twins say delightedly. They are sitting next to me while I dictate this quote, out loud, to my laptop. "Okayyyyy!" they continue, nodding knowingly, enthusiastically.

"If we resist aligning our interiors with the social order, we create openings into which we can spontaneously grow."[135]

"OK!" they say, nodding.

"Removing the social filter pushes us to explore what might have been possible, had we continued to believe that what is most beautiful is the moment when we are most ourselves. Even if that means being messy, vulnerable, or despairing—"[136]

"OK OK, OK!" both kids are rolling around, laughing.

"And *indeed*"—I raise my voice so I can be heard by the software—"to mobilise potential and to ensure

134. Nuar Alsadir, *Animal Joy: A Book of Laughter and Resuscitation* (London: Fitzcarraldo Editions, 2022), 17.
135. *Ibid.*
136. *Ibid.*

proper maturation, the child has to overcome many frustrations."[137]

"Ahhhh OK OK Okayyyy! OK OK OK!" They are screaming now, and in any case the transcription has stopped working.

> How can one study the emotional development of society?
asked Donald Winnicott in 1954.
> Such a study must be closely related to the study of the individual; the two studies must take place simultaneously.[138]

The eighteenth-century development of the liberal individual shaped a body and mind free to form and create itself, rather than be shaped by the dominance of church, state, feudal system, or tyranny. This free individual was the foundation of much twentieth-century thought and the founding principle of a free-market economy—a system in which economic decisions are guided by the interactions of individual citizens and businesses. After this system was adopted as a model by the Mont Pelerin Society in 1947, liberalism evolved into neoliberalism, a model based on ironclad self-sufficiency, competition, and enterprise, led by the rationality that the highest common good is for individuals to *self*-invest, *self*-create, and *self*-manage in ways that contribute to the appreciation (or at least prevent the depreciation) of their human capital.[139]

137. Perls, Hefferline, and Goodman, *Gestalt Therapy*, author's note.
138. Winnicott, *The Family and Individual Development*, 230.
139. An ethos that is well-documented by the entrepreneurial appreciation of Jay Z's famed lyric: "I'm not a businessman, I'm a business, man!" See Abdallah Alaili, *Entrepreneur Post*, March 12, 2023, https://www.entrepreneurpost.com/2023/03/12/im-not-a-businessman-im-a-business-man-jay-z/.

Neoliberalism leads to the disavowal of anything that is not "productive" in the narrow economic understanding of the term. It compounds life impulses into a degraded monoculture grown by the financial organisation of markets and intensively managed by shocks and anxieties.[140] Under the guise of improving societal conditions and with rapidly advancing technological progress, "men do not live their own lives but *perform* pre-established functions"[141] within "a citizenry left to its (manipulated) interests and passions."[142] To lesser or greater extents, and from different starting points, many countries found themselves adapting to neoliberalism for their domestic economies. "There is no alternative," declared Margaret Thatcher by 1981.

It seems bizarre that the health of the free market manifested in an image: a convoy of cardboard boxes carried by investment bankers ejected from an insolvent global financial services firm. On September 15, 2008, the 168-year-old investment bank Lehman Brothers, with $639 billion in assets, filed the largest bankruptcy in US history. This was a watershed moment in the Great Recession of 2007–09, in which the liquidity of financial markets contracted so savagely, triggered by an uncontrolled (and uncontrollable) international financial sector, that markets crashed worldwide. Twenty days later, across the Atlantic, when Alistair Darling, the UK's chief finance minister, received a phone call from

---

140. "A subject, construed and constructed as human capital both for itself and for a firm or state is at persistent risk of failure, redundancy and abandonment through no doing of its own, regardless of how savvy and responsible it is." (Brown, *Undoing The Demos*). Being a performing commodity is anxiety-inducing. Wendy Brown calls this condition "jeopardy."
141. Marcuse, *Eros and Civilization*, 44–45.
142. Brown, *Undoing the Demos*, 179.

the chairman of the Royal Bank of Scotland, the largest
bank in the world at the time (in assets) it was clear that
the market was very, very sick: "We are haemorrhaging
cash," said the chairman, who then continued to the truly
wretched part: "What are *you* going to do about it?"

A CEO posing such a question to a government
minister revealed a tectonic shift, having built up over
decades, during which Michel Foucault looked upon
the impending conditions and neatly preempted a new
world, where "the relationship defined by eighteenth
century liberalism is completely reversed."[143] Classical
liberalism is based on the state keeping its distance and
leaving the markets well alone, whereas neoliberalism

> activates the state on behalf of the economy,
> not to undertake economic functions or to inter-
> vene in economic effects, but rather to facilitate
> economic competition and growth and to
> economise the social,

or, as Foucault puts it, via Wendy Brown, to "regulate society by the market." Reflecting on this shift
Brown dives in further: "What might seem small at first
blush," she notes, "unfolds new worlds."[144] In this new
world, a state must "govern *for* the market."[145]

Anatomical, bodily metaphors have been used across
centuries to describe financial markets: descriptions
of balance, flow, stagnation, and circulation evoke
conditions of health or sickness. These metaphors become useful when the global financial market has reck-
lessly injured itself with its own impropriety, is bleeding
to death, is haemorrhaging cash and needs to be rescued.

---

143. Michel Foucault, *The Birth of Biopolitics: Lectures at
the Collège de France, 1978–79*, ed. Michel Senellart, trans.
Graham Burchell (London and New York: Palgrave
Macmillan, 2008), 121.
144. Brown, *Undoing the Demos*, 62.
145. Foucault, *The Birth of Biopolitics*, 121.

It was convenient—strategic perhaps—that the market be imaged on a human body, a powerful patriarch too big to fail, one who holds the most power and needs to be kept moving. It got under our skin—or, rather, it already *was* our skin, an authority, not good enough yet mighty enough to receive amnesty from self-annihilation after its debauched, decades-long ludomanic bender. Perhaps the best security against such risk might be for individuals to behave like markets. Yet imitating the leader does not bestow the follower the same privileges. After Darling and his global counterparts responded positively to phone calls from the biggest banks, it appeared that the state was working for the markets, but not for most individuals, who were kept in step, but always trailing behind.

The immediate cost of keeping the biggest banks liquid was €2.7 trillion within the Eurozone, eventually £850 billion in the UK, €360 billion in France,[146] and $700 billion in the United States. Since this appeared to come largely from government revenue—tax collected from individuals—and while on paper these bailouts were partly "paid back" over the following years, it created enormous deficits in the immediate present, which were corrected by longer-term austerity measures: reduced welfare spending, the cancellation of school building programs, reductions in local government funding. Such measures injured society because they targeted and harmed individuals.

146. See "Bank Reforms: How Much Did We Bail Them Out and How Much Do They Still Owe?," *The Guardian*, November 12, 2011, https://www.theguardian.com/news/datablog/2011/nov/12/bank-bailouts-uk-credit-crunch; Andrew Grice, "£850bn: Official Cost of the Bank Bailout," *The Independent*, December 4, 2009, https://www.independent.co.uk/news/uk/politics/163-850bn-official-cost-of-the-bank-bailout-1833830.html; and Antoine Lerougetel, "France: €360 Billion to Bail Out the Banks," *World Socialist Web Site*, October 20, 2008, https://www.wsws.org/en/articles/2008/10/fran-o20.html.

Around this time, novel tech industries broke ground, and a disembodied, unregulated media infrastructure started to form. An anti-establishment mistrust of political leaders and political representation opened up —coupled with a desire on both the far left and the far right to see the present system collapse. Immediately, anti-neoliberal and anti-establishment movements, including vibrant, collective forms of solidarity and direct action built momentum (for instance the Occupy movement). Simultaneously, under imposed austerity measures, individuals who had, for decades, consented to boom and behave with self-sufficiency—to invest in and set their human capital to work—were incapacitated, fueling disdain for the "neoliberal elite." This propagated the emergence of alternatives, ready to be mimicked, including populist, xenophobic leaders, and their ideologies.[147] Yet these leaders and their ideologies were saturated with the behaviours of neoliberalism itself: the desire for self-sovereignty and ironclad self-sufficiency[148].

In *Mothers: An Essay on Love and Cruelty* (2018), Jacqueline Rose recounts Virginia Woolf's thoughts on whether it is, without question, correct to place one's own child, and family, "before everyone else," and considers the damage such thinking might do to society.[149]

147. Brexit and the election of Donald Trump are often attributed to a delayed reaction to the 2008 financial crisis. See Andrew Grice, "Donald Trump and Brexit Have Proven the Centre Ground Is Dead—and the 2008 Recession Killed It," *The Independent*, November 9, 2016, https://www.independent.co.uk/voices/donald-trump-hillary-clinton-presidential-election-centre-ground-theresa-may-brexit-a7406786.html.
148. Everyone was dependent once, and may become dependent again. Ironclad self-sufficiency thrives when we erase our collective memory of our dependencies, ongoing.
149. Rose, *Mothers*, 79.

In a section of her 1937 novel *The Years*, Woolf suggests that while England may take pride in its differences to Nazi Germany, there might nonetheless be a link between the "egoism of the bourgeois family and the autocracy of statehood."[150] The grown-up grandson of a colonel observes a room of guests performing the usual etiquettes and habits, namely inquiring about one another's children, ultimately to foreground their own interests and bodies:

> My boy—my girl… they were saying. But they're not interested in other people's children, he observed. Only in their own; their own property; their own flesh and blood, which they would protect with the unsheathed claws of the primaeval swamp… one rips down the belly; or teeth in the soft fur of the throat…. How then can we be civilised?[151]

This primary state of relations, says Rose, reveals that the "intricacy and breadth of human possibility can be side-lined or crushed before it's even begun."[152]

In 1963 Hannah Arendt reported for the *New Yorker* on the trial of Adolf Eichmann, an SS officer and one of the major organisers of the Holocaust. The accused aggressor is documented critically by Arendt to be—despite his monstrous atrocities—a normal, habit-prone worker and family man.[153] It's her "banality of evil"

150. *Ibid.*
151. Virginia Woolf, *The Years* (1937), http://gutenberg.net.au/ebooks03/0301221h.html.
152. Rose, *Mothers*, 80.
153. "Half a dozen psychiatrists had certified him as 'normal'—'More normal, at any rate, than I am after having examined him,' one of them was said to have exclaimed, while another had found that his whole psychological outlook, his attitude toward his wife and children, mother and father, brothers, sisters, and friends, was 'not only normal but most desirable.'" Hannah Arendt, *Eichmann in Jerusalem*, rev. ed. (1963; repr., New York: Viking, 1964),

that critics stumble over most—the idea of Eichmann as someone who wished to work hard to perform pre-established functions that his job dictated, build his career, please his employer, supporting a wife and five children. Though critics have argued that Arendt was conned by Eichmann's conduct on the stand, it is understood that many in the Nazi Party were of the ilk he portrayed.[154] This is why his charade was convincing: unthinking, uncritical egoism, following the "facts," blindsided by a strong leader and disaffected by a crumbling economy. This was typical behaviour in the party, creating the darkest black holes.

Disenchanted with the 1970s French Socialist government and fed up with the limits that Marxism was placing on the mind, the body, and the political imaginary, Michel Foucault drafted *The Birth of Biopolitics*. These lectures were written for and delivered at the Collège de France in 1978–79, around the time Margaret Thatcher took the reins in the UK. The lectures weren't published in English until 2008, the year of the crash.[155]

Following the Gulag and Nazi National Socialism, Foucault—like many intellectuals—was concerned that any state with too much power was a menace. He used the lectures to philosophise on a model of governmentality that could provide individuals with liberal rights and freedoms, thus giving space for minority practices (such as his own—intellectual, homosexual, anti-Fascist).

https://platypus1917.org/wp-content/uploads/2014/01/arendt_eichmanninjerusalem.pdf.
154. For instance, Jennifer Schuessler, "Book Portrays Eichmann as Evil, but Not Banal," *New York Times*, September 2, 2014, https://www.nytimes.com/2014/09/03/books/book-portrays-eichmann-as-evil-but-not-banal.html.
155. Mitchell Dean and Daniel Zamora foreground this appropriate coincidence in *The Last Man Takes LSD: Foucault and the End of Revolution* (New York: Verso Books, 2021), 13.

He imagined this space could be held, potentially,
within a somewhat socialist rubric, while avoiding
the risk of socialism becoming an instrument of political
repression. Yet, the model he came to articulate, appreci-
ate, and in many respects ordain, was neoliberalism.

Walking with the twins, I notice that they're no longer
infants. They're loping about in puffer jackets, swinging
their arms, wearing their hair long. I think about how
they've been my material for the past four years and
wonder if it's as possible to write about children
as it is to write about babies… since babies…

"Were you a baby once?" my daughter interrupts my
dictation.
    "Yes."
    "Is this about you?"
    "No."

"Unless everyone is potentially put at risk it would be
impossible to 'secure' aggregate desire," says Zeynep
Gambetti in her 2022 essay "Immanence, Neoliberalism,
Microfascism: Will We Die in Silence?"

> It is only when social safety nets and constitu-
> tional guarantees against reducing individuals
> to manageable inert matter are systematically
> dismantled that 'risk' becomes productive.[156]

Led by the market, the state's responsibilities turn
to governing individual conduct through the "willing"
participation of the governed. For the market to work,
individuals must "consent" to performing, operating,
working, and consuming competitively, thus metabolis-
ing the free choice, risks, and insecurities of markets.

---

156. Zeynep Gambetti, "Immanence, neoliberalism,
Microfascism: Will We Die in Silence?," in *Deleuze and
Guattari and Fascism*, ed. Rick Dolphijn and Rosi Braidotti
(Edinburgh: Edinburgh University Press, 2022), 55.

By self-investing in the growth of their human capital
(which includes their offspring), agreeing for all to become "free," consensual, economic actors—performing
in a truly "true" market—individual behaviours are
modified, and the market is pleased.[157]

Around the late 1970s, taken by Stoic practices of anti-
quity, Foucault hypothesised that for some Greco-Romans
an ethical, and pleasurable life became societal via life-
long practices of care: self-reflection, seeking/ giving
counsel, risky frankness (truth-telling in debate), and
regularly checking in on one's ethical goals, as well as
on one's health, dreams, and mind. Through such practices, free Greco-Roman men could shape themselves

157. To ensure the public would consent to this new way of
life, the founders, at Mont Pèlerin, made their vision—neoliberalism—synonymous with freedom, and made freedom feel
like "common sense". By infiltrating popular culture they
could reshape public consciousness, so that individuals would
passively *consent* to this "common-sense" ideology of freedom
and thus consent to neoliberalism [see footnote 94]. Today, this
infiltration and hegemony, their legacy, continues: on a British
Airways flight to Chicago, consecutive adverts pop up in economy class before I watch *Barbie*. All promise "freedom." The
first advert: "The freedom to be there, the freedom to dream,
the freedom to say yes, the freedom to say no, freedom for
you, freedom for them, the freedom to do anything, the freedom to do nothing at all, invest in your freedom. Citizen by
Investment, St Kitts and Nevis. THE FIRST. THE FINEST."
... And the next: "For as long as you need unlimited data,
FREEDOM. Get your Holafly SIM today." In each advert, actors perform the role of leading and owning their (and their
family's) life and time, predominantly on the beach. As David
Harvey points out... "For any single way of thought to become dominant, a conceptual apparatus must be advanced
that appeals to our intuitions and instincts, to our values and
desires, as well as to the possibilities inherent in our social
world. If successful, this conceptual apparatus becomes so embedded in common sense as to be taken for granted and not
open to question." (Harvey, *A Brief History of Neoliberalism*, 5)

into prudent, responsible individuals, well able to balance pleasures with restraints. Foucault called this self-handling "care of the self," "technologies of the self," and "practices of freedom," since those who partook were never obliged to act this way by a higher authority. Instead, they freely consented to these practices. At this time, as Mitchell Dean and Daniel Zamora have noted in *The Last Man Takes LSD* (2021), Foucault was engaged in "limit experiences" in leather and S/M clubs, where taking risks, and hurting or becoming hurt, operates within firm parameters of consent.[158] It seemed that engaging with these etiquettes —enlarging self-knowledge between free and reasoned actors, knowing oneself and self-creating one's limits, in the face of risky, complex scenarios—was on his mind, and in his body, while he read up on the Greeks and thought about the free market. The conclusion he apparently drew is that the ancient methods of productive self-management and responsibilization may help pose a provocative question, one that is highly relevant to the creation of neoliberalism: Since a self-managed individual can reason and govern himself, must society be governed at all? Given that self-mastery is an *ability* that can also procure the highest social mobility and rewards, such questions contain one of Foucault's philosophical false moves: a failure to consider inequality.[159]

In *Animal Joy* (2022), psychoanalyst and poet Nuar Alsidir aligns threads of commonality between undergoing psychoanalysis and attending clown school. Both, in very different ways, present a means by which to smash through the sediment of socialisation built up in a human psyche, personality, and body. Such layering begins when an infant adjusts its behaviour to please its mother,

---

158. Dean and Zamora, *The Last Man Takes LSD*, 119.
159. A point that Dean and Zamora also make, though via a slightly different route, in *The Last Man Takes LSD*, 181.

"a survival mechanism at base, given the infant's dependency on the mother for its basic needs."[160]

A socialised self starts to develop, through this modification of behaviour, in performing for and pleasing an authority figure. A *false self*—a role—emerges, one that will please the mother, one that can become a blueprint for pleasing, say, an industry, or a market, later.

> Giving the mother what we know she will affirm trains us to develop a radar for what is wanted by other people, as opposed to tuning in to what is inside us. The result is a sense of alienation from ourselves that gets transmitted to others and is often rewarded, because it keeps the wheels turning without catches or snags.[161]

Conversely, the self that presents itself in the spontaneous gestures of an infant—the "true self," a Winnicottian term—can develop if a "good enough" mother is willing and able to affirm and accept that the throttling, poking, lap-wiggling gestures of this not-yet-socialised individual contain immense knowledge. Through clowning—playing—the stratification of socialisation in which an individual has habitually coated themselves over years, decades, is peeled back by reaching deep into the body, into expressions of failure, vulnerability, crying into a comic red nose[162], to reveal the spontaneous,

---

160. Alsadir, *Animal Joy*, 14.
161. *Ibid.*, 17.
162. On February 17, 2024, at 4.30 p.m., in *A Thesis On Spillage*, at Graham Foundation, Nuar Alsidir—poet, psychoanalyst and trained clown—read from her book *Animal Joy*. She pointed out, as we left the building, that similarly to how the psoas muscle seems to disappear when it's vibrant, loose, un-stagnated (given it no longer creates negative symptoms elsewhere), a red nose disappears when a clown is their "true self." In clown terms, a true self, is open, loose, messy, un-stagnated. On a true-self-clown, the clown and the audience stop noticing the nose.

undefined *true self*—that little one inside us, "the one who doesn't know how to drive but loves to drive."[163]

That is to say, that vibrant capacity for play that grabs me by the neck and the armpits contains the highest calibre of adult psychological truth: no productive use value, no desire for social reward, no status, no honour, no self-mastery. Perhaps if Foucault had seen children's play rather than adult play, we would have a very different *Birth of Biopolitics*. Or, to put it simply, if he'd only "let the little one drive."

Through a series of adjustments and alignments in the UK's governmental policies, from 1979 onward, individuals began to absorb—metabolise—markets in their bodies and minds. This conjugation arrived alongside a rapidly changing world of corporate and individual desire for "things" and experiences to consume, imaged by technology and media, driven by comparisons and competition.[164] Competition is not a natural game between individuals; it needs to be created "by an active governmentality."[165]

> Indeed, generating new forms of disposability
> is absolutely necessary for the functioning
> of neoliberal governmentality,

says Gambetti.[166] Thus, the stratification of society

It vanishes. That big red symptom disappears.

163. Alsadir, *Animal Joy*, 19.

164. "I can recognize it as a lost object of my own work, and I perceive a longing for it, too, in what Fred Sandback called 'pedestrian space': 'literal, flat-footed, and everyday,' where the work of art exists 'right there along with everything else in the world, not up on a spatial pedestal.' It was an idea, he wrote, full of 'utopian glimmerings of art and life happily cohabiting.'" Andrea Fraser, "Why Does Fred Sandback's Work Make Me Cry," *Grey Room* 22 (Winter 2005),42.

165. Foucault, *The Birth of Biopolitics*, 120.

166. Gambetti, "Immanence, Neoliberalism, Microfascism," 55.

"according to the competitive economic performances of its members" propels the risk of failure (of not-winning as much as winning).[167] [168] Quantified biological bodies thus become alike to any other commodity—that is to say, "in competition with all other commodities," so much so that the social body goes missing.[169] During a period when she "dropped out" of the art world, Lee Lozano wrote in her notebooks, in what reads like a spontaneous flow of conjugations:

> NYC: a decade of competitiveness. Where competition thrives friends can't exist. Must give up competitive game-playing (gets to be predictable anyway). . . . If let be motivated by natural affection for people it might save this emptiness. Competition → emptiness.[170]

167. Marcuse, *Eros and Civilization*, 44.

168. Inequality—the creation of competing capitals—becomes the engine of neoliberalism, a governmentality that has systematically failed to generate new wealth. Its modus is *redistributing* existing wealth to the wealthiest parts of society by removing the limits on how wealth is moved and handled. In doing so, a new economic class is created: class power is restored. This is decisive and deliberate. It is a menace that moves on behalf of the ruling powers. After WWII, in the US, the share of national income taken by the top 1 per cent of income-earners fell from a pre-war high of 16 per cent to less than 8 per cent. Thus, there was a very strong impulse to recover this percentage and the upper classes had to "move decisively to protect themselves from political and economic annihilation." (Harvey, *A Brief History of Neoliberalism*, 15). To create an upper class, one must create those who are not not in that class, and thus neoliberalism depends—unreservedly—on creating inequality.

169. Marina Vishmidt, "Bodies in Space: On the Ends of Vulnerability," *Radical Philosophy* 208 (Autumn 2020): 42.

170. Lee Lozano, entry for May 2, 1970 (edited January 31, 1972), in *Private Book 9* (New York: Estate of Lee Lozano and Karma Books, courtesy Hauser & Wirth, 2021), 3.

"What are you doing?" asks my daughter.

"I'm writing an essay," I tell her.

"What's an essay?"

"A text. No. Okay, I'm actually writing a book. In fact, no. I'm writing an essay."

"Ah!" Now she seems impressed. "An *essay*! What's it about?"

"Hmm." This is awkward. "Uh. It's partly about you? I think—"

I hesitate, trying to hide the screen, though she's only four and cannot read it. She might not like this. This is the problem with real life. She might one day, or even now, have no interest in being my "content." I wonder about all the children of writers who have become for better and/or worse the subjects in their parents' business, or equally the individuals whose business is founded on a parent identifying as "mother."

"I am a woman, I am a mother . . . and you won't take that away from me," shouted Giorgia Meloni from a podium in the full-throttle speech that helped bring her ultra-right-wing party to power in Italy, proving (to me at least) that it's easy to use motherhood as a currency, but that motherhood alone changes nothing.[171]

171. Addressing the World Congress of Families in Verona (recording subsequently removed by YouTube for violating community rules), Giorgia Meloni seamlessly—powerfully—admonishes same-sex families and gender neutrality. She advances the national "brand" on the axis of defending traditional, securitized familial values. The full quote: "I am Giorgia, I am a woman, I am a mother, I am Italian, I am Christian, and you won't take that away from me." See Isaac Chotiner, "'I'm a Woman, I'm a Mother, I'm Christian': How Giorgia Meloni Took Control in the Italian Election," *New Yorker*, September 28, 2022, https://www.newyorker.com/news/q-and-a/im-a-woman-im-a-mother-im-christian-how-giorgia-meloni-took-control-in-the-italian-election.

As I write this, I think about how I don't want to write this—how I'd so much rather be jumping into lecture theatres—those lamplit rooms where an intellectual strides in like he's diving into a swimming pool, delivers knowledge, speaks into a hundred tape recorders to five hundred student-disciples crammed into a hall that seats only three hundred, all hungry to consume radical theory, to hear knowledge speak its own truth to power.[172] The desire to transgress, to *separate*, is Western knowledge. It is a history of becoming individual, alone, separate from all dependencies. This is not my condition. This is not our condition.

After surviving an unknown illness that may have been bacterial bronchitis or a belated, undiagnosed nervous breakdown—caused by eighty-five years of grieving her mother's death and generational trauma of the Messina earthquake, offset by rearing three children and five grandchildren with little funds and phenomenal, joyful exuberance—my grandma's destiny has changed. She can walk no more than fourteen steps on a good day. Her usual technologies of resilience—moving furniture, rearrangement of rooms, feeding others—have ceased. Armchair empiricism reveals a chain reaction: immobility while hospitalised; a heart muscle that grew weak; a lymphatic drainage clogged; legs that need to be elevated always, and which cut and bleed at the slightest knock; lowered vitality; uncertainty; a scrambling of gut feelings; the constant presence of my mother or my aunt as carers in her home. The furniture stays in place and so does Grandma. She is confused that an electrician still has not been called to rewire all her light switches to ground level, so she can turn lights on and off herself

---

172. *The Birth of Biopolitics* has a prologue in which Foucault's 1978–79 lectures are alluringly described in this way by his "disciples" philosopher François Ewald and historian, Alessandro Fontana.

from her armchair. While the twins hold her knitting needles like horns, marching up and down the stairs, or cover themselves in tangled pieces of brightly coloured wool, I crouch next to her to discuss the irrational/rational light-switch issue, but she changes the subject, telling me with conviction, urgently: "I have done very well. *Everyone* is doing very well. Nobody died."

If it was two thousand years ago, and I was a free Greco-Roman man, the Stoics would argue that if I looked after my "self," my body, my mind, my dreams, I would be better at looking after others. This might be true, or it might not be true. They wouldn't know. Caring for others is often attached to having absolutely no choice. There is no choice since if you choose to break with this duration, you will drop the multiple individuals you are holding and handling and they will fall, and they will break. Responding with a *recognition* of vulnerability—of *a* body, or bodies *alone*—while it remains increasingly unclear when the counter-praxis edges of a social body begin and end, is not enough.[173] Holding up, making buoyant, maintaining life over one's own and others' lifetimes is steadfast social praxis; yet, it is *so* collectively damaged. "It's as if genuine neediness—being or having been the baby of a mother—is what conservative rhetoric hates the most," Jacqueline Rose surmises,

> Perhaps when right-wing politicians screw up their noses at scroungers, asylum seekers and refugees, it is their own vaguely remembered years of utter dependency that they're instructing us to repudiate. The one who most loudly promotes the ideal of ironclad self-sufficiency must surely have the echo of the baby in the nursery hovering somewhere at the back of his or her—mostly his—head.[174]

---

173. Vishmidt, "Bodies in Space," 42.
174. Rose, *Mothers*, 30.

The easy part is saying what's wrong. The hard part
is saying what world you want to see. "We are in the
ultimate duration," says my boyfriend as he folds our
twins' freshly laundered clothes. There is no happy ending here, because there is no end. It is best to remain
pragmatic. It is hard to know how to finish. Critique
drops out easily. The request for a banana with a top
bitten off, the need to pay attention to a bruised leg,
or a binocular injury, or a child bouncing on one leg
because the other leg got hurt by the binoculars—plus
the dazzling vivacity of a ninety-six-year-old grandma
—is harder to bring in.

> Moments when the original 'poet' in each of us
> created the outside world for us, by finding the
> familiar in the unfamiliar,
>
> says Marion Miller,
>
> are perhaps forgotten by most people; or else
> they are guarded in some secret place of memory
> because they were too much like visitations by
> the gods to be mixed with everyday thinking.[175]

"How are we going to stop him being a badger?"
my daughter asks me after she has exited a two-hour
session of being pursued by her brother, who is still
crawling around on all fours, sniffing in corners, omni-
potently picking up slippers and trousers with his mouth.
He is a blur, an untranscribable apparition, as economi-
cally immeasurable as holding and handling life—
and which, similarly, is taking "all the fucking time."[176]

---

175. Marion Miller, *On Not Being Able to Paint* (1950;
repr., London and New York: Routledge Taylor and Francis
Group, 2010).
176. Mierle Laderman Ukeles, "MANIFESTO FOR
MAINTENANCE ART, 1969! Proposal for an exhibition:
'CARE,'" 1969, https://queensmuseum.org/wp-content/up-
loads/2016/04/ Ukeles-Manifesto-for-Maintenance-Art-
1969.pdf.

His sister has exited the visitation, for now, matter-of-fact.

"He can't be a badger forever."

She shakes her head.

For an impulse to emerge spontaneously from its passions, the impulse needs to be hooked up with the body and its "lewdness, idleness, systematic disposition of one's vital energies,"[177] that is to say, with all daily life and its dependencies, temperaments, temperatures, and needs: a wild, embodied knowledge that endures and exists. I try to grab him, get involved, tickle him maybe, but he's scuttled under the bed.

177. Federici, "Capitalism and the Sexual Division of Labor."

*A Hypothesis of Resistance,** by Cally Spooner

Five essays, edited and annotated in conversation with Will Holder. Initially published as *A Hypothesis of Resistance*, in Mousse Magazine:

Part One: "Asynchronicity," Mousse #81 – Fall 2022
Part Two: "Rehearsal," Mousse #82 – Winter 2023
Part Three: "The Present Tense," online at moussemagazine.it/magazine/the-present-tense-cally-spooner-2023
Part Four: "Undetectability," Mousse #84 – Summer 2023
Part Five: "Duration," Mousse #85 – Fall 2023

Publishing Editor: Agnese Cantelmi
(Mousse Publishing)

Copyediting for Mousse Magazine:
Antonio Scoccimarro, Chiara Moioli,
Madeleine Paré, Giulia Celuppi, Emma Passarella
Proofing for Mousse Magazine: Lindsey Westbrook

Copyediting and typesetting: Will Holder
Final proofreading: Janine Armin
Printing: TRT, Tallinn

Cover: Cally Spooner, *Screen Test for the Psoas Muscle*
(Installation view, Graham Foundation, Chicago, 2023)
Existing internal walls, CSP-1180 semi-gloss paint,
white emulsion paint, water, applied with horizontal,
vertical, and circular movement by Aske Thiberg.
Environmental dimensions

Published and distributed by
Mousse Publishing – Contrappunto srl
via Decembrio 28, 20137 Milan, Italy
moussemagazine.it

First edition: 2024
ISBN: 978–88–6749–642–6 € 18 / $ 20

A Hypothesis of Resistance was written alongside a series
of live events, producing shared, embodied knowledge,
outlined over the following pages:

ASYNCHRONICITY—a symposium-like-gathering
May 7 & 8, 2022
Kölnischer Kunstverein, Cologne
and Ludwig Forum for International Art, Aachen

Programmed by Cally Spooner with Eva Birkenstock, Nikola
Dietrich and Viktor Neumann. With: Paul Abbott & Will
Holder, Alex Baczynski-Jenkins, Taina Bucher, Elizabeth
Freeman, Hendrik Folkerts, Irena Haiduk, Dana Luciano,
Martina Roß-Nickoll, Cally Spooner with Sanna Blennow
& Melody Giron, Mark von Schlegell, Jesper List-Thomsen,
Jackie Wang and films by Pierre Bal-Blanc and Frances Scholz

ASYNCHRONICITY responded to the neoliberal paradigm
of measurable 'performance' by unraveling the resistant potentials of becoming or remaining asynchronous. Over the course
of two days, collaborators unfolded a diverse set of propositions for alternative, fugitive temporalities, affects and bodily
practices that bend and subvert familiarity and which deliberately, or naturally, remain out of sync, colliding these proposals
across the partnering institutions in Aachen and Cologne.
ASYNCHRONICITY was the final project of *reboot:
responsiveness*, the first cycle of *reboot:* a collaborative, multi-
cycle, anti-racist and queer-feminist dialogue encompassing
performance and research based practices jointly presented
by Viktor Neumann and

Kölnischer Kunstverein
Hahnenstraße 6, D - 50667 Köln
www.koelnischerkunstverein.de
Director: Nikola Dietrich

Ludwig Forum Aachen
Jülicher Str. 97-109, D - 52070 Aachen
www.ludwigforum.de
Director: Eva Birkenstock

`reboot: responsiveness` was funded by Kunststiftung
NRW and Stiftung Kunstfonds Neustart Kultur

DEADTIME Talks—editorial events
Between 20th June 2022 and 29th October 2023
O—Overgaden, Copenhagen

Programmed by Cally Spooner and Rhea Dall, *DEADTIME*
took place over a year and investigated how "performance"
has come to govern the entire realm of our social bonds,
and asked: how might this governance be resisted?

Each talk fluctuated between live performance, casual conversation, and academic content to build an ongoing local conversation on our present and pervasive "performance" condition. The final event, "Duration," aptly stretched to become a workshop, an event, and an exhibition.

"Asynchronicity", June 20, 2022.
With Will Holder, Rhea Dall, Cally Spooner,
and Jesper List Thomsen

"Rehearsal", November 24, 2022.
With Will Holder, Rhea Dall, Cally Spooner,
and Andreas Führer

"The Present Tense", December 15, 2022.
With Will Holder, Rhea Dall, Cally Spooner,
Marie Lund, and Irena Haiduk

"Undetectability", March 23, 2023.
With Will Holder, Rhea Dall, and Cally Spooner

"Duration", August 26–October 29, 2023.
An exhibition by Cally Spooner with Maggie Segale

O—Overgaden
Overgaden neden Vandet 17, 1414 Copenhagen, Denmark
https://overgaden.org
Director: Rhea Dall

UNDETECTABILITY—a symposium-like-gathering
March 21, 2023
Royal Danish Academy of Fine Art, Copenhagen

Programmed by Cally Spooner with Maibritt Borgen
in the Laboratory for Art Research. With: Sanna Blennow,
Maibritt Borgen, Taina Bucher, Cabaret Économique,
Nanna Debois Buhl, Hendrik Folkerts, Will Holder,
Rune Hjarnø Rasmussen, Cia Rinne, Jenny Gräf Sheppard,
Cally Spooner, and Kristin Veel.

UNDETECTABILITY unfolded on the first day of a new lunar phase. From twilight (18.25) till just past midnight (00.01), propositions for darkness, invisibility, and blindness were tested at the Royal Danish Academy of Fine Art. While the moon was undetectable to the naked eye, participants from dance, art, academia, cabaret, poetry and magic proposed methods to resist hyper visuality and detection. The Laboratory for Art Research

Royal Danish Academy of Fine Arts,
Kongens Nytorv 1, 1050 Copenhagen, Denmark
https://kunstakademiet.dk/en/laboratory-art-research
Acting Head: Maibritt Borgen

A THESIS ON SPILLAGE—*a symposium-like-gathering*
February 17, 2024
Graham Foundation for Advanced Studies in the Fine Arts,
Chicago

Programmed by Cally Spooner and Hendrik Folkerts.
With: Nuar Alsadir, Marquis Bey, Wendy Brown, Joshua
Chambers-Letson, Tony Cokes, Hendrik Folkerts, Melody
Giron, Irena Haiduk, Sarah Herda, Darrell Jones, Sanford
Kwinter, Ralph Lemon, Maggie Segale, Cally Spooner,
and Frances Stark.

A THESIS ON SPILLAGE unfolded as a diverse set of
proposals for 'spillage'—philosophical, artistic, psychoanalytical, practical, choreographic. Each defied and eclipsed the
drive for individual and societal bodies to perform to-wards
a metric-orientated future; a future which represses anything
that cannot be quantified, instrumentalized, tracked, or rated.

A THESIS ON SPILLAGE was the opening event to
(and took place within) *DEADTIME*—*an anatomy study*,
Cally Spooner's Graham Foundation Fellowship exhibition,
including sound, film, sculpture, painting, installation, and
five essays entitled *A Hypothesis of Resistance*—installed over
the three floors of galleries at the historic Madlener House.

DEADTIME—*an anatomy study* was co-curated by
Graham Foundation director, Sarah Herda and Hendrik
Folkerts, curator of international contemporary art and
head of exhibitions at Moderna Museet, Stockholm,
with Graham Foundation program and communications
manager Ava Barrett.

Graham Foundation for Advanced Studies in the Fine Arts
Madlener House, 4 West Burton Place,
Chicago, Illinois 60610 USA
www.grahamfoundation.org
Director: Sarah Herda

A Hypothesis of Resistance
has been generously supported by

novo nordisk **fonden** — The Novo Nordisk Foundation's Mads Øvlisen PhD scholarship for practice-based research

Graham Foundation — Graham Foundation for Advanced Studies in the Fine Arts, Chicago

Danish Arts Foundation

OVERGADEN — O—Overgaden, Copenhagen

KÖLNISCHER KUNSTVEREIN — Kölnischer Kunstverein

Ludwig Forum Aachen — Ludwig Forum Aachen

STIFTUNG KUNSTFONDS — Stiftung Kunstfonds

Kunststiftung NRW — Kunststiftung NRW

Thank you to the co-organisers of the live events:
Eva Birkenstock, Nikola Dietrich & Viktor Neumann
with Hermann Müller; Maibritt Borgen; Sarah Herda
with Ava Barrett. Thank you Hendrik Folkerts for co-organising and for *DEADTIME*, the entirety within
which this book sits; and Rhea Dall for three years
hosting *DEADTIME*, *A Hypothesis of Resistance*.

Thank you Antonio Scoccimarro, Chiara Moioli
and all at Mousse Magazine; and to Gloria Di Risi.

Special thanks to Will Holder, Jesper List Thomsen,
Franca and Hedi List, Angela Spooner
and Maria Wojtanowski née Crucitti.

ISBN 978–88–6749–642–6